W9-BTJ-961

INSIDE PURGATORY

BT
832
.P475
2000

INSIDE PURGATORY

What History, Theology and the Mystics Tell Us about Purgatory

THOMAS W. PETRISKO

AVE MARIA UNIVERSITY

St. Andrew's Productions

CONSECRATION
AND DEDICATION

This book is consecrated to the Merciful Heart of Christ. It is dedicated to Fr. Richard Whetstone, a most faithful servant of our Father.

St. Andrew's Productions

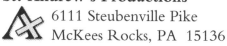
6111 Steubenville Pike
McKees Rocks, PA 15136

Copyright © 2000 by Dr. Thomas W. Petrisko
Second Printing 2002
ISBN 1-891903-24-1
All Rights Reserved

Toll-Free: (888) 654-6279
Phone: (412) 787-9735
Fax: (412) 787-5204

Web: www.SaintAndrew.com

Scriptural quotations are take from The Holy Bible —RSV: Catholic Edition. Alternate translations from the Latin Vulgate Bible (Douay Rheims Version —DV) are indicated when used. Some of the Scriptural quotations from the New American Bible: St. Joseph Edition, The New American Bible— Fireside Family Edition 1984-1985, The Holy Bible—Douay Rheims Edition, The New American Bible— Red Letter Edition 1986.

PRINTED IN THE UNITED STATES OF AMERICA

ACKNOWLEDGMENTS

I wish to thank those most helpful to me during the writing of this book: Dr. Frank Novasack, Fr. Richard Whetstone, Fr. Bill McCarthy, Michael Fontecchio, Amanda DeFazio, Carole McElwain, and the prayer group at the Pittsburgh Center for Peace.

I thank my family for the support and sacrifice they have made for this work, my wife Emily, daughters Maria, Sarah, Natasha, Dominique and my sons, Joshua and Jesse. As always, a special thank you to my mother and father, Andrew and Mary Petrisko and my uncle, Sam.

ABOUT THE AUTHOR

D r. Thomas W. Petrisko was the President of the *Pittsburgh Center for Peace* from 1990 to 1998 and he served as the editor of the Center's nine "Special Edition" newspapers. These papers, primarily featuring the apparitions and revelations of the Virgin Mary, were published in many millions throughout the world.

Dr. Petrisko is the author of seventeen books, including: *The Fatima Prophecies, At the Doorstep of the World; The Face of the Father, An Exclusive interview with Barbara Centilli Concerning Her Revelations and Visions of God the Father; Glory to the Father, A Look at the Mystical Life of Georgette Faniel; For the Soul of the Family; The Story of the Apparitions of the Virgin Mary to Estela Ruiz, The Sorrow, the Sacrifice and the Triumph; The Visions, Apparitions and Prophecies of Christina Gallagher, Call of the Ages, The Prophecy of Daniel, In God's Hands, The Miraculous Story of Little Audrey Santo, Mother of The Secret, False Prophets of Today, St. Joseph and the Triumph of the Saints, The Last Crusade, The Kingdom of Our Father, Inside Heaven and Hell and Inside Purgatory and Fatima's Third Secret Explained.*

The decree of the **Congregation for the Propagation of the Faith** (AAS 58, 1186 – approved by Pope Paul VI on 14 October 1966) requires that the *Nihil Obstat* and *Imprimatur* are no longer required for publications that deal with private revelations, apparitions, prophecies, miracles, etc., provided that nothing is said in contradiction of faith and morals.

The author hereby affirms his unconditional submission to whatever final judgment is delivered by the Church regarding some of the events currently under investigation in this book.

TABLE OF CONTENTS

FOREWORD

by Fr. Richard Foley, S.J.

As we have come to expect from Dr. Petrisko, he presents us with an in-depth wide-ranging treatment of the subject – matter. Which, in this his latest book, is Purgatory. He gives us the equivalent of a guided tour of Gods holy penitential world where human spirits are purified and thereby prepared for entry into Paradise. Thus readers will find an abundance of information about Purgatory. At the same time they will find in Dr. Petrisko's book plenty of inspiration and encouragement to become more Purgatory minded; that is, generous in offering spiritual succour and support to the Holy Souls.

The notion of indispensable spiritual purification before going into God's presence is, of course, a tradition as old as religion itself. But in Christianity its true meaning has been progressively developed under the action of the Holy Spirit. So much so, indeed, that Purgatory, as well as that closely-related truth known as the Communion of Saints, both now enjoy dogmatic status. In the 16th century these doctrines were comprehensively dealt with by the Council of Trent as part of its task of countering the heretical views of the so-called reformers; they taught, among other things, that Christ's merits dispense us from the necessity of expiatory suffering in purification, whether in this world or in the next, on account of our personal sins.

Dr. Petrisko directs onto his subject many a spotlight coming from various authorities down the Christian centuries – popes, theologians, saints, mystics and visionaries. Together their insights in testimonies present a rounded picture of that mysterious realm of purgatorial pain and prayer, which can be likened to Heaven's vestibule lying beyond this world.

As is so often the case when examining faith's mysteries, it is the saints and mystics who shed much helpful illumination. Any number of them have been privileged to behold Purgatory, thus learning something of its set–up and the sort of sufferings the Holy Souls must endure; in some instances they were even allowed to converse with them.

Notable among these mystics was St. Catherine of Genoa; what impressed her most of all was the perfect conformism of God's holy will on the part of the suffering souls and their deep-seated peace. Moreover, they fully appreciate that their penitential pain is in fact a precious grace from the All-Holy, who has decreed that nothing defiled shall enter Heaven.

St. Teresa of Avila's mystical experiences of Purgatory generated in her an immense compassion and charity towards its suffering inmates and a resolve to do all she could to bring them succour and solace. Indeed, she was often divinely enlightened to see how her prayers had served to liberate some of them and transport them to Heaven. St. Mary Magdalen of Pazzi frequently had a similar experience. And St. Margaret Mary learned from certain souls in Purgatory how it's specific punishments match the kind and degree of particular sins and imperfections. As for St. Catherine of Sienna, she won from God the grace to suffer in her own body what her own father still had to endure in Purgatory; he was instantly released, and, radiant with heavily joy, appeared to her to express his deep gratitude for what she had done.

As regards the duration factor in Purgatory, St. Robert Bellarmine was convinced that its sufferings are not limited to a maximum of 10 or 20 year, as was commonly held; rather, they are to be reckoned in some cases as lasting an entire century. And as for the severity of purgatorial suffering, St. Thomas Aquinas held that the least particle of its pain even exceeds everything the Saviour had to endure during His passion. This view was endorsed by St. Mary Magdalen of Pazzi; in comparison with Purgatory's torments, she's on record as saying, "the dungeons of the martyrs are gardens of delight."

As we would expect, the Mother of God plays a prominent role in the lives of her many children who are prisoners of divine justice in God's austere kingdom of penitence and purification. It was revealed to St. Peter Damien that on each annual feast of the Assumption thousands of Holy Souls are released at our Lady's intercession.

In modern times it is not least at Medjugorje that the Queen of Purgatory has repeatedly and strikingly displayed her maternal compassion and zeal with regard to the Holy Souls. Besides teaching us much about Purgatory itself, she urges us to offer prayers and suffrages for the relief, if not the released, of our suffering brothers and sisters. For example, one of her messages reads (November 6, 1986):

"Dear children, today I invite you to pray daily for the souls of Purgatory. Prayer and grace are needed by each soul for it to reach God and his love. By doing this you will win for yourselves new intercessors who will help you to realize that all earthly things are unimportant, and that we should strive only to reach heaven. Therefore pray without ceasing so as to benefit both yourselves and those to whom your prayers will bring joy."

Fr. Richard Foley S.J.
London
February 24, 2000

INTRODUCTION

Today there is little mention of Purgatory, even among Catholics. It is, however, a teaching handed down from the Apostles and found in Sacred Scripture.

Purgatory is said to be a necessary part of the justice of God, which responds to all sin. The Church teaches that even the least sin displeases God. Thus, His mercy, which pardons, contains His justice, which cleanses. Purgatory, therefore, is a place of justice.

Many saints have witnessed and written about this transitory state. It is, in many ways, a frightening place, yet unlike Hell, it contains peace and hope. In Purgatory as in Hell there is a double pain—the pain of loss and the pain of the senses. The pain of loss consists of being temporarily deprived of the sight of God, Who is the supreme good, the beatific end for which our souls are made. This is a moral thirst that torments the soul's love for God. The pain of senses is similar to what we experience in our flesh.

Although its nature is not defined by the (Catholic) faith, the Doctors of the Church believe this world of suffering is primarily in a foggy, misty place of darkness, a vast area said to be ash gray and cloudy with different levels, some fiery. The lowest levels are said to hold great suffering.

Saint Lydwine of Schiedam, who died in 1433, wrote of such places from her own experiences in ecstasy. Upon seeing this lowest level of Purgatory, Saint Lydwine saw what appeared to be walled pits in an immense prison of fire. She inquired of her guide, an angel, "Is this then Hell, my brother?" "No, sister," replied the angel, "but this part of

Purgatory is bordering on Hell."

The upper levels of Purgatory are said to be more calm and tranquil, as if almost in Heaven. These abodes are said to be near Heaven and filled with greater light.

Regardless of what level, souls are said to hunger to leave, to depart for Heaven in order to finally see God. Like earthly prisoners, the souls in Purgatory long to be released from their sadness, captivity, and suffering. They want to get out and they need us to help them.

Saint Catherine of Siena, in order to spare her father the pains of Purgatory, even offered herself to Divine Justice to suffer in his place. Not surprisingly, God accepted her offer. It is said that from this Saint Catherine suffered the rest of her life till death, but her father was set free. Like Saint Catherine, we are also in a position to help release souls. We just need to take action on their behalf.

May all who read this little book come to know the truth about Purgatory, how each of us face the possibility of going there if not purified of the stain of our sins before death, and how the countless souls there are waiting for our help to get them into Heaven.

Chapter One

PERFECTION THROUGH PURIFICATION

O f all the afterlife realms, none is more controversial and misunderstood than Purgatory. Simply defined, Purgatory is a place of purification, a transitory region designated for souls who die in a state of grace but who aren't pure enough to enter Heaven. But what exactly occurs there? And why should Christians believe in it?

The history of Purgatory is somewhat vague and seems to be a synthesis of ancient beliefs, biblical tradition, and for Christians, evolving doctrine. According to scholars, the term "purgatory" did not exist until the 12th century, after which it's usage quickly became common. Dante Alighieri included it in his *Divine Comedy*. However, it was not until the mid-13th century that the Catholic doctrine of Purgatory became an official teaching of the Church.

But Purgatory's roots in Scripture were known and its tradition in the Church discernible from the very beginning. To support this, theologians cite the inscriptions found on the walls of the caves and catacombs of the early Christians. These markings confirm the early concept of Purgatory and prove that the Christian custom of praying for the purification of the dead has existed for at least 20 centuries. We also find the foundation for this Catholic belief in the writings of the early Church Fathers. Many of them wrote that "some" souls, after death, still needed purification before entering Heaven.

Today, Catholic doctrine on Purgatory is supported by both Tradition and Scripture and is an article of the faith upheld by many Popes in their pastoral teachings. In 1994, the most recent Catholic Catechism defined the doctrine of Purgatory: "From the beginning the

Church has honored the memory of the dead and offered prayers in suffrage for them, above all the Eucharistic sacrifice, so that, thus purified, they may attain the beatific vision of God."

The Church also commends almsgiving, indulgences, and works of penance undertaken on behalf of the dead. St. John Chrysostom provides a Scriptural basis for this Catholic belief:

> Let us help and commemorate them. If Job's sons were purified by their father's sacrifice, why would we doubt that our offerings for the dead bring them some consolation? Let us not hesitate to help those who have died and to offer our prayers for them.

This reference by St. John Chrysostom to the Old Testament story of Job is significant because it establishes that a rudimentary doctrine of Purgatory existed prior to the birth of Christ. However, evidence suggests that the practice of assisting the dead on their journey to Heaven is even older than the story of Job.

According to scholars, ancient heathens similarly believed in an afterlife place of expiation. This belief stemmed from a universal concept of a supreme being, who because of his perfection, required purification of his creatures before allowing them into his presence. Expiatory sacrifices for the dead existed in those cultures that adhered to this concept of afterlife purification. Chinese, Carthaginean, Japanese, Egyptian, Slav, Persian, Celtic, Greenlander, and even American Indians shared the belief that after death, a soul must endure and undergo trials that demonstrate its worthiness for entering the dwelling place of the supreme being and that assistance from the living was most helpful and appreciated by the dead. This assistance included prayers, holocausts, and cremations, offerings placed on graves and tombs, elaborate funeral ceremonies, and other practices of atonement.

Expiation practices developed because it was thought that some souls at death were obviously too good for Hell but not good enough for Heaven, or too corrupt for Heaven but not evil enough for Hell. Many cultures integrated into their belief systems a place of cleansing between Heaven and Hell for such individuals, regardless of whether they were heretics, infidels, criminals, or those deluded by false logic or sinful ways.

For example, the Greeks and the Romans developed elaborate customs to aid their deceased ancestors. In his works, Plato explained the Greek concept of purgation:

> As soon as the departed have arrived at the place to which they are conducted by demons, the separation of the just and holy from the wicked takes place. Those found to have led nearly a good life are conducted to the Great Lake to dwell there and atone for their faults till they are absolved. They whose condition is judged to be beyond remedy because of the wickedness of their transgressions, are plunged into Tartarus, whence they are never released. They whose faults have been great, but remedied to some degree, are also plunged into Tartarus; but after remaining a year, the waves throw them ashore and they are transferred back to the Sea of Acherusia. If they are received there by them against whom they offended, their punishment is ended. They, however, that shall be found to have made great progression in holy life, escape all these prisons in the interior of the earth, and proceed to the pure abode above the earth.

Plato also wrote on the judgment of souls after death:

> Separated from their bodies, souls come at once before the judge who examines them with care. If he finds one disfigured by faults, he sends it to the place where it will suffer the punishments it has merited. Some among these souls profit by the punishments which they endure since their faults can be expiated. Pain alone delivers them from injustice. But those who committed great crimes and whose perversity is incurable, can serve only as examples.

Plato's reasoning was the same as many saints of the Catholic Church, including Aquinas and Catherine of Genoa: the divine order of the afterworld, like the temporal order, must be regulated by penial compensation. If a soul acknowledges and accepts its penalty, it is permitted to re-enter the order it has violated.

The Roman poet, Virgil, believed that souls after death were unable to free themselves of the vices they accumulated while in their bodies and, consequently, a place was needed for them to expiate these faults through pain and sufferings. The Romans used to recite special prayers for the dead and invoke the aid of celestial spirits: "Come to our aid, O' Heavenly Spirits...take care of his (her) soul and have great pity." After sealing the tomb, they would invoke for their loved one: "May you be happy soon and forever." Father John Laux refers to ancient Egyptian, Persian, and Greek concepts of after-death purification in his book *Chief Truths of the Faith*:

> A purification of souls after death was known to several pagan religions, such as the Egyptian and the Persian. Plato speaks of souls that have to be cleansed in the river Acheron, because on earth they led but indifferent lives; and of others that have to pass a year in Tartarus (Hell) before they can attain to perfect happiness. He makes a clear distinction between *curable* and *incurable* offenses.

Jewish tradition also called for the friends and families of the dead to pray for their loved ones so God would shower mercy on their souls. Indeed, the Jews believed and trusted in God's fairness and justice and revered his holiness. In The book of Wisdom, we read that "nothing defiled can come into the presence of the Spirit of Wisdom" (Wis 7:25). It is especially noted how the Old Testament reveals this through God's actions, and that although forgiveness of sins by God is obtained, divine justice, nevertheless, demands satisfaction for the remitted sins. Temporal punishment is rightly due and justly given.

In The book of Wisdom God "brought Adam out of his sin," but Adam still had to cultivate the soil by the "sweat of his brow." With Moses and Aaron, denial of the promised land served as expiation. Likewise, David is forgiven, but the death of his son is required as punishment: "The Lord hath taken away thy sin. Nevertheless, because thou hath given occasion to the enemies of the Lord to blaspheme, thy child shall surely die" (2 Sam 12:14).

As with the Jewish doctrine of Heaven, belief in justice after death emerged over time and was developed through the writings of the prophets. By the 2nd century BC., the concept of an afterlife for the Jews expanded to include the belief that a person was judged after death according to their earthly works and deeds and that the prayers of the living would help temper the justice given to a soul.

Theologians note that Christ registered no protest against this Jewish doctrine and teaching. In 2 Maccabees 12:39-46, authored in the 2nd century BC, we read that "it is therefore a holy and wholesome thought to pray for the dead that they may be loosed from sins." We also read in Maccabees how Judas Maccabeus, "making a gathering, sent twelve thousand drackmas of silver to Jerusalem for sacrifice to be offered for the ...dead...who had fallen asleep with godliness...that they may be loosed from sins." Moreover, throughout the Old Testament (Job. 4:11, 12:9; Ecclus 3:33; Dan. 4:24), we read that almsgiving delivers the dead from the pain and suffering of sin.

Scholars note how in *The Book of Samuel* the deaths of Jonathan, Saul, and Abner required the people to fast for an entire week, believing this had a purifying effect on their souls (1 Sam 31:13). In Genesis, we read how the Patriarch Joseph, upon his father's death, holds a mourning celebration of 70 days and a funeral of 7 days. This same concept is found when the dying Tobias says to his son, "Place your bread on the tomb of the righteous, and gather the poor around it to eat and drink" (Tob 4:17).

Theologians say Tobias said this because he believed acts of charity would purify departed souls. Likewise, the prophet Micheas takes comfort in trusting in such a place of purification: "I will bear the wrath of the Lord because I have sinned against Him until he judges my case and executes judgement for me" (Mic 7:9). Finally, in Ecclesiasticus, we read, "A gift hath grace in the sight of all the living; and restrain not grace from the dead." According to Fr. Garrigou Lagrange, this passage showed that according to the faith of Israel "the just, after death, could be aided by the sacrifices offered on earth."

Scholars note that although the Jews of this period weren't certain where souls went to be purified, they did believe in a temporary period of expiation in Hell or a similar abode in Sheol. According to author Charles Panati in his book, *Sacred Origins of Profound Things*

(Penguin, 1996), the school of Jewish theology headed by the Rabbi Shammai "explicitly taught that expiation of sin from a soul is accomplished in the blast furnace of Hell."

No theology of Purgatory was ever formally established by the Jews, but in the rabbinical literature of the 1st century AD, Gehenna, or Hell, is described as a place where souls of the dead are purified before continuing on to Heaven. According to some rabbis, this belief was discerned from the writings of Zechariah, "And I will bring the third part through the fire and will refine them as silver is refined; and I will try them as gold is tried" (Zech 13:9). Likewise, the writings of Isaiah are said to speak of such a purifying place for the souls of the deceased: "The people that walked in darkness have seen a great light, to them that dwelt in the region of the shadow of death, light is risen" (Is 9:2).

In his reflection on Purgatory on August 4, 1999, Pope John Paul II explicitly states how the Old Testament writings of the Jews establish the need for a process of purification before a soul is worthy to enter into perfect communion with God:

> According to Old Testament religious law, what is destined for God must be perfect. As a result, physical integrity is also specifically required for the realities which come into contact with God at the sacrificial level such as, for example, sacrificial animals (cf. Lev. 22:22) or at the institutional level, as in the case of priests or ministers of worship (cf. Lev. 21:17–23). Total dedication to the God of the Covenant, along the lines of the great teachings found in *Deuteronomy* (cf. 6:5), and which must correspond to this physical integrity, is required of individuals and society as a whole (cf. 1 *Kings* 8:61). It is a matter of loving God with all one's being, with purity of heart and the witness of deeds (cf. ibid., 10:12f.).
>
> The need for integrity obviously becomes necessary after death, for entering into perfect and complete communion with God. Those who do not possess this integrity must undergo purification.
>
> At times to reach a state of perfect integrity a person's intercession or mediation is needed. For

example, Moses obtains pardon for the people with a prayer in which he recalls the saving work done by God in the past, and prays for his ancestors (cf. Ex 32:30, 11-13). The figure of the Servant of the Lord, outlined in *The Book of Isaiah*, is also portrayed by his role of intercession and expiation for many; at the end of his suffering he "will see the light" and "will justify many," bearing their iniquities" (Is 52: 13-53, 12, especially 53:11).

Psalm 51 can be considered, according to the perspective of the Old Testament as a synthesis of the process of integration: The sinner confesses and recognizes his guilt, asking insistently to be purified or cleansed" (Ps 51:2, 9, 10, 17) so as to proclaim the divine praise.

The Jews so believe in the doctrine of purification in the next world that they still stress, through their customs, the defense and practice of it. For example, if a child's father is deceased, the child is encouraged to recite for a whole year a specific prayer called "Kaddish" for his/her deceased father. If there are no children, strangers are compensated for saying this ancient prayer.

The Jewish faith also perpetuates the ancient tradition of lighting candles for the dead. These are called "Yortise candles." Along with the Jewish tradition of almsgiving, the ritual act of praying for the dead at the Wailing Wall in Jerusalem exists even to this day. There, before the world, the practice of praying for the dead is visible for all to see.

For the Jews, perhaps the concept of Purgatory is best defined in the words of the Psalmist: "Justice and peace have kissed."

Chapter Two

PURGATORY: A DOCTRINE FOUND IN SCRIPTURE

In Catholic Doctrine, it is standard teaching that certain verses of the New Testament can be undeniably asserted as evidence in support of the doctrine of Purgatory. While troublesome for Protestants, these passages for Catholics establish an undisputed truth of the faith—that there is a middle state, called Purgatory, for those souls who leave this world justified in the eyes of God, but who need final purification in order to be reunited with Him. This doctrine is twofold in application, for it embraces not only the souls who depart this world and enter temporarily into Purgatory, but also the living who, the Church teaches, can help such souls hasten their release from Purgatory.

The following New Testament passages provide the most authoritative support for Catholic doctrine on Purgatory:

> *Mt 12:32* — "Whoever speaks against the Holy Spirit, it will not be forgiven him, either in this world or in the world to come." [With these words, according to Sts. Augustine, Gregory the Great, Bernard, and many more, it is clearly revealed that forgiveness is obtainable in the next world. And since that forgiveness cannot come in Heaven or Hell, because of the nature of each, there leaves only one possibility—these sins are forgivable in Purgatory.]
>
> *Mt 5:25-26* — "Lose no time, settle with your opponent while on the way to court with him. Otherwise your opponent may hand you over to the judge, who will hand you over to the guard, who will

throw you into prison. I warn you shall not come out from *it* until you have paid the last penny." [With this specific teaching of Christ, concerning temporal as well as spiritual debt, the pronoun *"it"* is clearly understood by theologians to imply Purgatory, and that release from this "spiritual prison" is contingent upon a soul's complete payment of retribution to divine justice for its sins. St. Jerome, Origen, St. Ambrose, and others stated that this passage not only refers to eternal punishment in the next world but also of atonement there.]

 2 Tim 1:18 — "May the Lord grant him to find mercy from the Lord on that day." [According to theologians, St. Paul's prayer for Onesiphorus infers a third place, a place where the soul after its earthly trial, can find mercy. This passage hints that although a soul is not in Heaven, it still has a chance to get there.]

 1 Cor 3:13-15 — "The work of each will be made clear. The day will disclose it.

 That day will make its appearance with fire, and fire will test the quality of each man's work. If the building a man has raised on this foundation still stands, he will receive his recompense, if a man's building burns, he will suffer loss. He himself will be saved, but only as one fleeing through fire." [The Fathers of the Church wrote that the fire spoken of here is the purifying fire of Purgatory, which tests all men's work to see if they are gold or silver, or, in essence, purified.]

While some may argue that these Scriptural passages do not directly address the question of Purgatory, there is considerable evidence that the early Church did not suffer from such a dilemma. Moreover, Tradition is clearly on the side of belief in a purification after death and that the custom of praying for the dead was a universal practice of the faithful from the very beginning.

Indeed, in the subterranean tombs of the early Christians, the caves and catacombs of Rome and Palestine, there is impressive evidence remaining of faith in the power of prayer to help one's departed loved ones. A number of well known cemeteries in Rome that date back to the first three centuries reveal numerous inscriptions such as: "Here, dearest son, thy life has come to an end. But thee, O' Heavenly Father, we implore to have mercy, to take pity on the sufferings of our dear one, through Christ, Our Lord," and, "To Lucifera, whosoever of the brethren chances to read this, let him pray to God to take unto Himself her holy and pure spirit," and, "Eternal light shine upon thee, Timothea, in Christ."

In fact, hundreds of such inscriptions are traceable back to the early Church, as Fr. John Laux explains in his book, *Chief Truths of the Faith*:

> [On] tombs in the first three centuries, both in the Catacombs and elsewhere, we find the phrases, "May God refresh thee," and "Mayest thou have eternal light in Christ." We find the same words used in the Church's prayer for the dead: "Be mindful, O Lord, of they servants N. and N., who are gone before us with the sign of faith, and sleep in the sleep of peace. To them O Lord and to all who sleep in Christ, grant, we beseech Thee, a place of refreshment, light and peace, through the same Christ our Lord."

St. John Chrysostom, in his *Third Homily*, discusses how the Church Fathers clearly upheld the doctrine of Purgatory in their writings:

> The apostles did not ordain without good reason a commemoration of the departed to be made during the celebration of the sacred mysteries; for from it the deceased draw great gain and help. Why should our prayers for them not placate God, when, besides the priest, the whole people stand with uplifted hands whilst the August Victim is present on the altar? True, it is offered only for such as departed hence in the faith." Wrote St. Gregory of Nyssa: "The apostles and disciples of Christ have handed down to us what since has obtained the force of law everywhere in the Church of God, namely that the memory of those that died in the

true faith be recalled in the celebration of the sacred and
illustrious mystery.

In his funeral oration over the Emperor Theodosius the Great,
St. Ambrose of Milan (1397) prayed, "Give rest to Thy servant,
Theodosius, that rest which Thou hast prepared for Thy saints....I have
loved him, and therefore will I follow him unto the land of the living;
not will I leave him until by tears and prayers I shall lead him whither
his merits summon him, unto the holy mountain of the Lord.

In the 2nd century, Tertullian wrote that "on the anniversary of
the dead we offer the Holy Sacrifice for the departed. Even though
Scripture did not warrant this, the custom originates in Tradition, it was
confirmed by universal adoption and sanctioned by faith." He also
wrote, "We make oblations for the dead one year after their death."

In the 3rd century, we find from the touching accounts of the
martyr, St. Perpetua, a similar endorsement of the faith in the doctrine
of Purgatory. Perpetua prayed for her brother Dinocrates and, in vision,
saw his pain gradually lessened until he finally appeared to her in a full
luminous, countenance: "I then awoke," writes Perpetua, "and knew
that my brother's punishments were over."

In the 4th century, St. Jerome wrote of the value of prayers and
alms over tears for the dead, while St. Epiphanuis, St. Ambrose, Origen,
St. Basil, St. Cyril of Jerusalem, and St. Gregory the Great all concurred
with the tradition. Echoing Scripture's words, St. Gregory the Great
spoke of a purifying fire and the forgiveness of sins, even after death:

> As for certain lesser fruits, we must believe that before
> the final judgement, there is a purifying fire. He who is
> truth says that whoever utters blasphemy against the
> Holy Spirit will be pardoned neither in this age nor in
> the age to come. From this sentence, we understand
> that certain offences can be forgiven in this age, but
> certain others in the age to come.

St. Ephrem wrote of the need for remembrance of the dead on
the 13th day after death, while St. Cyril of Alexandria believed that
prayers made for the dead obtain succor for them. He also wrote about
the expiation of sins after death.

After the 4th century, texts refer specifically to the doctrine of Purgatory and even of the belief of fiery punishments undergone by the just who have not sufficiently expiated their sins in their lifetimes. Sts. Augustine, Caesarius Arles, and Gregory the Great affirm four truths which contain the entire doctrine of Purgatory:

1) After death, there is no longer a possibility of merit or demerit;

2) Purgatory exists and is a place where souls undergo temporary pains for their sins;

3) These souls can be aided by the prayers of those who live, especially the Sacrifice of Mass;

4) Purgatory will end on the day of judgement.

Most noted are the words of St. Augustine, the 4th century Father and Doctor of the Church, who devoted the ninth book of his *Confessions* to an account of the final days of his mother, St. Monica:

> When the day of her dissolution was at hand, she took no thought to have her body sumptuously wound up, or embalmed with spices, nor desired she a choice monument, or to be buried in her own land. These things she enjoined us not; but desired only to have her same commemorated at Thy Altar, from which she knew that Holy Sacrifice to be dispensed, by which the handwriting that was against us is blotted out.... May she, then, rest in peace with her husband... And thou, O Lord, my God, inspire thy servants my brethren, whom with voice, and heart, and pen I serve, that so many as shall read these confessions may at the altar remember Monica, thy handmaid with Patricus, who was once her husband.

Over the centuries, the liturgy for the dead was gradually formed and a string of Church councils continued to vindicate the doctrine of Purgatory, beginning with the Council of Carthage which recommended prayers for the dead, as did the Roman Synod in 502. The Synod of Orleans in 533, the Council of Braga in 563, the

Council of Toledo in 675, the Synod of Chalons in 813, and the Synod of Worms in 868 all maintained that belief in Purgatory was a sound teaching of the faith. Finally, the First and Second Councils of Lyons (1245 and 1274) declared in 1274 that "the Holy Roman Church declares and teaches that when truly penitent souls die in charity before they have atoned for their faults of commission and omission by worthy fruits of penance, they are purified in the torments of Purgatory."

In the 14th century, the Council of Florence (1439) established that "souls in Purgatory are benefitted by the suffrages (prayers) of the living faithful, namely the Sacrifice of the Mass, prayers, alms, and other works of piety." A century later, the Council of Trent (Session VI. 22, 25.) declared firmly that the faithful are able to assist the souls detained in Purgatory by their prayers and the Holy Sacrifice of Mass, and that anyone teaching contrary to the doctrine of Purgatory may be threatened with excommunication:

> The Catholic Church, instructed by the Holy Ghost, has from the Sacred Scriptures and the ancient traditions of the Fathers, taught in Sacred Councils, and very recently in this Ecumenical Synod, that there is a Purgatory, and that the souls therein detained are helped by the suffrages of the faithful, but principally by the acceptable Sacrifice of the Altar.

The Church Catechism resulting from the Council of Trent urged priests to teach this truth of the faith:

> Among them is also the fire of purgatory, in which the souls of just men are cleansed by a temporary punishment, in order to be admitted into their eternal country, into which nothing defiled entereth. The truth of this doctrine, founded, as holy Councils declare on Scripture, and confirmed by Apostolic tradition, demands exposition from the pastor, all the more diligent and frequent because we live in times when men *"endure not sound doctrine."*

Centuries later, Vatican II urged the pious memory of the dead.

In *Lumen Gentium*, we read that "it is a holy and wholesome thought to pray for the dead that they may be loosed from their sins."

Therefore, for Catholics, the reality of Purgatory is incontestable. As St. Robert Bellarmine stated, "The doctrine of the existence of Purgatory is so Catholic a dogma that they who nevertheless deny it assuredly have to fear not Purgatory, but rather the flames of Hell."

Chapter Three

THE PAINS OF PURGATORY

The beatified 20th century Italian mystic, Padre Pio, reportedly said that he saw so many souls from Purgatory that "they don't frighten me anymore." His words, though understandable in light of his status as a mystic, are still perplexing because we cannot see these souls. Despite this, however, we need to understand why souls are in Purgatory and what their true condition is. What exactly is lacking in a soul departing this world that remits it to Purgatory? And what exactly do souls experience there to satisfy divine justice?

According to common Church doctrine, souls who die in a state of grace, yet are not pure enough to enter Heaven, are sentenced to a place, an abode, of temporal punishment. These souls are not pure enough because the consequences of forgiven mortal and venial sins remain on their soul. Although this "residue" adheres to the soul like rust on iron, it is less obvious on a soul in grace. According to theologians, this "rust" is easy to retain since even the slightest imperfection, the slightest degree of self-love is contrary to the pure love of God. At death, therefore, any degree of pride or desire for happiness from this world is a weight upon a soul that needs to be lifted.

We need to remember, though, that a soul does not have to be exceptionally evil to need Purgatory. In life, souls have every opportunity to repent, but once life is over, no further repentance can occur. Purgatory is not a place of repentance, but for purification.

The Catholic Church does not define the precise nature of the punishment or the mode of purification that a soul receives in Purgatory. Nor does the Church teach exactly where Purgatory is located or how long a soul must stay there. Nevertheless, common beliefs and teachings addressing these issues have been handed down.

According to Tradition, once the course of a person's life is over, the time of mercy and merit is over, too. God becomes our judge. Delivered before the throne of God by angels, as both St. Aquinas and St. Bonaventure believed, a soul is sentenced and goes to the abode decreed by divine justice.

If saved, a soul enters Purgatory with limited knowledge, as it is generally believed that such souls have knowledge only of the affairs that pertain to them. These souls, Tradition teaches, may not pray for themselves and must rely on the intercessory prayers of the living. The souls in Purgatory retain certain faith, hope, and charity. And although they cannot yet fully contemplate God, they do have an infused measure of divine love, corresponding to merit.

Despite their inability to pray for themselves, the suffering souls in Purgatory can pray for others and implore God to deliver them. They can also, it is believed, invoke the aid of the faithful. According to some saints, the suffering souls even console each other as permitted by God.

Most importantly, the souls have no fear since they know they have been preserved from damnation. However, according to Tradition, they suffer depending on their sanctity and the degree of justice imposed upon them by God. Resigned to this suffering, souls experience neither terror or confusion but patience, which according to many sources, is a peaceful state of suffering with the great hope of the future glory that is to be theirs.

According to theologians, the sufferings of Purgatory are twofold: (1) the delay of the beatific vision and (2) the pain of the senses.

The Delay of the Beatific Vision

The delay of the beatific vision is the pain a soul must endure in Purgatory—the pain of being separated from the One the soul now seeks to be with in a new and most passionate manner. As Fr. Garrigou Lagrange writes in *Life Everlasting,* this suffering is the primary pain of Purgatory and cannot be compared to any suffering on earth:

> Privation of the beatific vision is painful in the same degree as the desire of that vision is vivid. Two reasons, one negative, the other positive, show the vividness of this desire.

Negatively, its desire for God is no longer retarded by the weight of the body, by the distractions and occupations of this terrestrial life. Created goods cannot distract it from the suffering it has in the privation of God.

Positively, its desire of God is very intense, because the hour has arrived when it would be in the enjoyment of God if it had not placed thereunto an obstacle by the faults which it must expiate.

The souls in purgatory grasp much more clearly than we do, by reason of their infused ideas, the measureless value of the immediate vision of God, of His inadmissible possession. Further, they have intuition of themselves. Sure of their own salvation, they know with absolute certainty that they are predestined to see God, face to face. Without this delay for expiation, the moment of separation from the body would coincide with that of entrance into heaven.

In the radical order of spiritual life, then, the separated soul ought already to enjoy the beatific vision. Hence it has a hunger for God which it cannot experience here on earth. It has failed to prepare for its rendezvous with God. Since it failed to search for Him, He now hides Himself.

Analogies may be helpful. We are awaiting, with great anxiety, a friend with whom to discuss an important matter at a determined hour. If our friend is delayed, inquietude supervenes. The longer the delay, the more does inquietude grow. In the physical order, if our meal is retarded, say six hours or more, hunger grows ever more painful. If we have not eaten for three days, hunger becomes very severe.

Thus, in the spiritual domain, the separated soul has an insatiable hunger for God. It understands much better than it did on earth that its will has a depth without measure, that only God seen face to face can fill this will and draw it irresistibly. This immense void renders it more avid to see the sovereign good.

This desire surpasses by far the natural desire, conditional and inefficacious, to see God. The desire of which we speak now is a supernatural desire, which proceeds from infused hope and infused charity. It is an efficacious desire, which will be infallibly fulfilled, but later. For the moment God refuses to fulfill this desire. The soul, having sought itself instead of God, cannot now find Him.

Joy follows perfect activity. The greatest joy, then, follows the act of seeing God. The absence of this vision, when its hour has arrived, causes the greatest pain. Souls in purgatory feel most vividly their impotence and poverty. A parallel on earth appears in the saints. Like St. Paul, saints desire to die and to be with Christ.

We often hear it said that in the souls' purgatory there is an ebb and flood. Strongly drawn toward God, they are held back by the "remains of sin," which they have to expiate. They cannot rush to the goal which they so ardently desire. Love of God does not diminish their pain, but increases it. And this love is no longer meritorious. How eloquent is their title: the suffering Church!"

St. Catherine of Genoa, in her *Treatise on Purgatory*, offered the following analogy to help better explain the suffering associated with the delay of the beatific vision in Purgatory:

Let us suppose in the entire world only one loaf of bread. Further, even the sight of this loaf would satisfy the hunger of every creature. Now man, in good health, has by nature the instinct of nourishment and hence the pain of hunger. If he could abstain from eating without losing health and life, his hunger would cause an ever more intolerable pain. If therefore man were certain he would never see this unique loaf of which we have spoken, his hell would be something like that of the damned. Now the souls in purgatory have the certain hope of seeing this unique loaf and of being entirely sated by it. But they endure an ever increasing pain of hunger until they enter into the eternal possession of this bread of life, which is Jesus Christ, our Lord.

The Pain of the Senses

According to Tradition, the souls in Purgatory experience a pain of the senses, although they no longer have a body. Besides the pain of sorrow, chagrin, and shame of conscience, which most theologians admit all souls in Purgatory suffer, there is the almost universal recognition of pain associated with the purifying fire of Purgatory. This fire is different from the fire of Hell, but is a real fire and must be classified as a sensory experience for the souls.

This belief has been supported and promoted over many centuries by nearly all the Fathers and Doctors of the Church and is also found, theologians say, in Corinthians I. Private revelations, too, have contributed over the centuries to sustained belief in this teaching.

Fr. Lagrange explores how fire could possibly cause pain in souls separated from their earthly, material bodies:

> Fire is an instrument of justice, as baptismal water is an instrument of grace. A soul which has refused the instruments of mercy must suffer from the instruments of justice.
>
> The mode of this action remains mysterious. This fire has the power to bind the soul, that is, to hinder it from acting as it would and where it would. It inflicts on the soul the humiliation of depending on a material creature. An analogy is seen in paralyzed persons who cannot act as they would.

Likewise, St. Augustine addressed purgatorial pain in *De Civitate Dei, Book XXI*:

> If the fire be not immaterial like the pain of the soul, but material, causing us to smart only when we touch it, then the question may be asked: how can it

constitute a punishment for spirits?

It is not necessary to engage in a long disputation or argument on this question. For that prohibits us to believe that spirits can be made sensitive albeit in a miraculous manner, of a material fire, when the spirit of man, which is truly immaterial, can be inclosed in the human body dying natural life and after the day of judgement? The spirits, then, though having no body, will be bound to a material fire, experiencing pain from it, but giving it no nourishment. For also that other manner by which spirits are now joined to bodies, is truly wonderful and above the conception of man, and yet it is what constitutes man. I might say the spirits burn without having a body, the same as Dives burned in hell when he exclaimed, "I am tormented in this flame"....But that hell, which is called by Scripture a lake of fire and brimstone, shall be material fire as was declared by eternal truth.

In *Caring for the Suffering Souls*, Reverend John A. Nageleisen summarizes what St. Thomas and others in the Church, including Popes and mystics, have agreed on regarding the fire of Purgatory:

Theologians, with St. Thomas, teach that by divine co-operation fire exerts its influence on the souls physically and really; it confines the soul to a certain space, and limits its activity there in a manner most violent and unnatural. The pain of sense, then, consists principally in a purifying, material fire. Although the suffering souls are designed for heaven, they are nevertheless denied admission there because in the heavenly Jerusalem only the purest and finest gold is accepted. The Suffering Souls, though gold, are still defiled by the dross of the earth from which they were created. Therefore the Lord detains them in a fiery furnace, there to purify them, like unrefined gold, of all dross and spurious material. "And He shall sit refining and cleansing the silver, and He shall purify the sons of

Levi and refine them as gold and as silver." (Mal.3:3.)

This fire is a most fierce, penetrating, and all-consuming flame; a fire whose power immeasurably exceeds the strength of natural fire; a fire which causes infinitely greater pain than all pains, torments and penitential works of this world; for the souls are no longer limited in their power of endurance by the body, which can suffer only to a certain degree without succumbing. The Latin Church, through Pope Eugene and the Fathers of the Council of Florence, was about to declare as a dogma that the fire of Purgatory was a material one, because this was and is the continual belief of the church; but in order to facilitate the union between the Latin and Greek Churches, this declaration was deemed inopportune, the Greeks declaring their belief in Purgatory, "but we do not argue whether it consists in fire, darkness or tempest;" and for the sake of peace the Council was content with this declaration. At all events the discussion served to establish clearly the Church's belief in Purgatory.

The existence of fire in Purgatory is vouched for also by numerous apparitions and private revelations. They demonstrate to our very eyes this fire as a material one, thus indicating that the words "fire" and "fiery torments" used by Scripture are to be taken in a literal sense. St. Bridget, of whom the Church, in her official prayer, says, "O God, who through Thy Divine Son didst reveal to blessed Bridget heavenly mysteries," was permitted in one of her ecstasies to witness how a soul was sentenced to a three-fold punishment: to an external and internal fire, an intense cold, and to furious assaults of the devil.

Mechtildis of Magdeburg saw a lake of fire mixed with brimstone, in which the Suffering Souls had to bathe in order to be cleansed. According to St. Frances of Rome Purgatory consists of three apartments, one above the other, all with a clear, sparkling fire, unlike that of hell, which is dark and

somber.   [Regarding] Venerable Mary Anna
Lindmayer: "Her friend Mary Becher and her mother
appeared to her and left marks of fire on one of her feet,
which she saw and felt for weeks. At one time she
beheld Purgatory in the shape of a torrent of fiery water,
at another, as a prison of fire. The souls themselves
appeared to her as sparks of fire falling about her. The
appearance of some souls caused her to shiver with frost
caused by cold proceeding from them."

With the sole exception of their duration, the
torments of Purgatory are the very same as those of hell;
the only difference is that the former are temporary, the
latter everlasting. This is the doctrine of St. Thomas,
who says: "The same fire punishes the damned in hell
and the just in Purgatory, and the least pain in Purgatory
exceeds the greatest we can suffer in this world."

Theologians note that it is not certain whether any other modes
of purification exist in Purgatory, but many believe there are other
afflictions such as cold, darkness, occasional fear induced by evil spirits,
filth, heavy work loads, hunger, odors, thirst, and specific afflictions
associated with the purgatory of specific sins. But, regardless of the type
of purification, explains St. Thomas Aquinas, souls accept them
voluntarily:

In the sense that the soul wills to bear them, as benefits
imposed upon it by divine justice, it realizes the
suitableness of this vivid plan, to purify the depths of the
soul, to erase all egoism and self-seeking. The soul,
though it had not courage during life to impose upon
itself this deep interior suffering, now accepts that
suffering voluntary.

While no one can say how long a soul must stay in Purgatory it
is generally recognized that time in this spiritual domain moves
relatively slow. Many private revelations depict time in Purgatory to be
exponentially greater than an equivalent period of time on earth.
Likewise, it is believed that for some souls, the duration of time in

Purgatory can be quite lengthy. At Fatima, the Virgin Mary said that a certain soul, when asked about by the visionaries, was to remain in Purgatory till the end of the world. Fr. Lagrange explores the concept of time in Purgatory:

> But if the question regards the duration of purgatory for a particular soul, we can but answer that the punishment will be longer and more intense according to the expiation required. Suffering corresponds to guilt, and its duration corresponds to the root of sin. Thus one soul may suffer long, but with less affliction than another, whose more intense affection brings earlier deliverance.
>
> Let us illustrate by an analogy. Punishment on earth, say scourging, may be severe and brief, whereas imprisonment may be long and less severe. In the spiritual order, too, penance for a grave sin may be brief and severe, while for faults less grave but more deeply rooted, it may be long and mild....Souls converted at the last moment, after a life of grave disorder, remain in purgatory much longer then ten or twenty years. Theological opinion, in general, favors long duration of purgatorial purification. Private revelations mention three or four centuries, or even more, especially for those who have head high office and great responsibility.
>
> Perhaps to totally understand the unique nature of suffering in Purgatory, one must realize that no soul would depart Purgatory without having paid its full dues, for the souls in Purgatory actually desire to serve their sentence and to fulfill divine justice to the letter. St. Frances de Sales writes of this truth:
>
> It is true that the torments of Purgatory are so great that the most acute sufferings of this life cannot compare to them, but the interior satisfaction which is enjoyed is such that no prosperity, no contentment on earth, can equal it. The souls are in continual union with God. They are perfectly resigned to His Will, or rather,

their will is transformed into that of God, so that they cannot will but that which He wills, Indeed, if paradise were to be opened to them, they would precipitate themselves into Hell rather than appear before God with the stains with which they see themselves disfigured. They willingly and lovingly purify themselves, because such is the divine pleasure.

And so, through the purifying fire of Purgatory—God's loving and merciful justice—souls not yet pure enough for Heaven are transformed into a more perfect "image of God."

Chapter Four

VISITATIONS FROM THE SOULS

The Catholic Tradition of Purgatory, perhaps more than that of Heaven and Hell, is reinforced by private revelation, especially so called "apparitions of the dead." These accounts, stories, and legends form a rich part of the lives of the saints, with many of the Church's heroic figures of the past revealing, through mystical experiences, the "reality" of Purgatory.

Often noted are detailed accounts of souls detained in Purgatory who are reportedly permitted to appear on earth to plead for prayers, sacrifices, Masses, and other forms of holy assistance to relieve their sufferings. Deceased relatives, friends, religious, and even famous people are said to have come back to, not only ask for help, but to shed light on the purpose and experience of Purgatory.

Accounts of Purgatory have also been offered by individuals who have either "visited" there in some mystical fashion or were shown Purgatory in a dream or vision. Like the other accounts, these reports are captivating and together form a rich compendium of information concerning Purgatory.

While such revelations do not belong to "Divine Revelation", they have been generally regarded over the centuries as providing reliable truths, especially when they come from saints and religious. Theologians advise that people can use such revelations to seek greater enlightenment on Purgatory and that it is not inappropriate or sinful. They explain that through private revelation, God, seeks to multiply the evidence of His truths, which in turn strengthens belief in the mysteries of the faith.

So what exactly have the Saints and other chosen souls revealed over the centuries about Purgatory?

In summary, the mystical accounts of Purgatory are very consistent with Church doctrine, although in some there is a difference of perception in the types of purification and the severity of the suffering.

However, theologians have upheld these revelations, especially with regards to severity and duration in Purgatory. The saints say it is a fact that souls who convert at the last moment, after leading rather sinful lives, are reasonable candidates for longer or more intense purification. This reasoning is also compatible with revelations that disclose levels or types of Purgatory. The lower levels are said to be closer to Hell and, consequently, more like Hell in their forms of purgation. While upper levels, being closer to Heaven, reportedly share more in what Heaven is like, although still administering to the souls a degree of purification.

Most stories of Purgatory do not reveal its extremes. Rather, the typical account is of a suffering soul who comes back to someone he knew in this life to plead for assistance. Often forming in a mist, a light, or a shadow, the suffering soul will appear out of nowhere and incite compassion (or dread) from their surprised benefactors. Some are said to have sad, imploring countenances, and wear garments of mourning. Other souls materialize enveloped in flames or wrapped in chains. Most appear to be in the midst of suffering, a condition betrayed by their moans, sobs, pleas, painful words, or hurried and deep sighs. Often the souls will be repentant or try to confess, offering regrets for their past mistakes to the witnesses. All are seeking deliverance.

The proposed environments of Purgatory are as diverse as the types of sufferings. In visions and dreams many souls have appeared in what looks like a dungeon, or a prison cell, others in dark, foggy, swamp-like surroundings. Some have appeared in pits and cauldrons of boiling liquids. Whether or not these are symbolic or metaphorical states is unknown. Souls in higher states of Purgatory have also been seen in different ways. They appear in locales such as roads, towns, and villages that are similar to earth, as well as ethereal meadows and fields that suggest Heaven.

But perhaps the best way to illustrate the realism of these accounts of Purgatory is to examine the stories. Therefore, in the next chapter, a sampling of these revelations is offered in an effort to demonstrate God's merciful justice after death.

Chapter Five

PURGATORY AND THE SAINTS

B ecause the Church places considerable importance on Tradition, revelations of the saints are considered to have great merit. Throughout the history of the Church, private revelations of Purgatory have been recorded by saints such as St. Teresa of Avila, St. Gertrude the Great, St. Magdalen de Pazzi, St. Thomas Aquinas, St. Margaret of Cortona, St. Brigetta of Sweden, St. John Vianney, St. Francis of De Sales, St. Lidwina of Schiedam, St. Margaret Mary Alacoque, St. Nicholas of Tolentino, St. Catherine of Siena, St. Philip Neri, St. John Bosco, Bl. Padre Pio, and Saint Faustina Kowalska—to name but a few.

Most noted are the revelations of St. Catherine of Genoa, who because of her *Treatise on Purgatory*, is considered to be the most authoritative saint on the subject. For centuries, St. Catherine of Genoa's treatise has been recognized as the most revealing work ever written on the subject. The treatise explores the attitude of the souls in Purgatory, their sufferings, how and why they choose to go to Purgatory of their own volition, and how the sins people expiate in this life have a much smaller price than they do after death in Purgatory.

St. Catherine of Genoa writes that the souls in Purgatory have no choice but to be there, as God has ordained it in his justice. These souls, she said, retain no knowledge of why they are in purgatory and are content with their disposition since they are desirous only of pleasing God. At their judgement they see why they are going to Purgatory, but never again while there.

In Purgatory, St. Catherine saw that the souls there experience great peace, and that this peace increases as they are being purified. The fire of Purgatory, she emphasized, consumes all the stains of the soul,

AVE MARIA UNIVERSITY

until all such defects are gone. But although their torments are great, the souls desire only to satisfy God.

St. Catherine said she also saw that the source of all suffering in Purgatory is either original sin or actual sin. But because these souls have an assured hope of seeing God and since this end is only precluded by Purgatory, they embrace their purifications regardless of how intense. Thus, the slightest imperfection becomes something a soul urgently seeks to remove. Souls, St. Catherine tells us, perceive Purgatory as a truly great grace from God:

> This process of purification to which I see the souls in Purgatory subjected, I feel within myself, and have experienced it for the last two years. Every day I see and feel it more clearly. My soul seems to live in this body as in a Purgatory which resembles the true Purgatory, with only the difference that my soul is subjected to only so much suffering as the body can endure without dying, but which will continually and gradually increase until death.
>
> I feel my spirit alienated from all things (even spiritual ones) that might afford it nourishment or give it consolation. I have no relish for either temporal or spiritual goods through the will, the understanding, or the memory, nor can I say that I take greater satisfaction in this thing than in that.
>
> I have been so besieged interiorly, that all things which refreshed my spiritual or my bodily life have been gradually taken from me, and as they departed, I learned that they were all sources of consolation and support. Yet, as soon as they were discovered by the spirit they became tasteless and hateful; they vanish and I care not to prevent it. This is because the spirit instinctively endeavors to rid itself of every hindrance to its perfection and so resolutely that it would rather go to Hell than fail in its purpose. It persists, therefore, in casting off all things by which the inner man might nourish himself, and so jealously guards him, that no slightest imperfection can creep in without being

instantly detected and expelled.

As for the outward man, for the reason that the spirit has no correspondence with it, it is so oppressed that nothing on earth can give it comfort according to its human inclinations. No consolation remains to it but God, who, with great love and mercy accomplishes this work for the satisfaction of His justice. I perceive all this, and it gives me a great peace and satisfaction; but this satisfaction does by no means diminish my oppression or my pain. Nor could there possibly befall me a pain so great, that it could move me to swerve from the divine ordinance, or leave my prison, or wish to leave it until God is satisfied, not could I experience any woe so great as would be an escape from His divine decree, so merciful and so full of justice do I find it.

I see these things clearly, but words fail me to describe them as I wish. What I have described is going on within my spirit, and therefore I have said it. The prison which detains me is the world; my chains, the body; the soul, illuminated by grace, comprehends how great a misery it is to be hindered from her final end, and she suffers greatly because she is very tender. She receives from God, by His grace, a certain dignity which assimilates her to Him, nay, which makes her one with Him by the participation of His goodness. And as it is impossible for God to suffer any pain, it is so also with those happy souls who are drawing nearer to Him. The more closely they approach Him the more fully do they share in His perfections.

Any delay, then, causes the soul intolerable pain. The pain and the delay prevent the full action both of what is hers by nature, and of that which has been revealed to her by grace; and, not able as yet to possess and still essentially capable of possessing, her pain is great in proportion to her desire of God. The more perfectly she knows Him, the more ardent is her desire, and the more sinless is she. The impediments that bear her from Him become all the more terrible to her, because she is so wholly bent on Him, and when not one of these is left she knows Him as He is.

As a man who suffers death rather than offend God does not become insensible to the pains of death, but is so illuminated by God that his zeal for the divine honor is greater than his love for life, so the soul, knowing the will of God, esteems it more than all outward or inward torments, however terrible; and this for the reason that God, for whom the work is done, is infinitely more desirable than all else that can be known or understood. And inasmuch as God keeps the soul absorbed in Himself and in His majesty, even though it be only in a slight degree, yet she can attach no importance to anything beside. She loses in Him all that is her own, and can neither see nor speak, nor yet be conscious of any injury or pain she suffers, but as I have said before it is all understood in one moment as she passes from this life. And finally, to conclude all, understand well, that in the almighty and merciful God, all that is in man is wholly transformed and that Purgatory purifies him.

St. Teresa of Avila

St. Teresa of Avila, one of only three female Doctors of the Church, reported many mystical insights on Purgatory. She had great charity towards the suffering souls and God often showed her how the power of her prayer worked toward the delivery of souls into Heaven. St. Teresa described a particular vision she had of several such souls:

I received tidings of the death of a religious who had formerly been Provincial of that province, and afterwards of another. I was acquainted with him, and he had rendered me great service. This intelligence caused me great uneasiness. Although this man was commendable for many virtues, I was apprehensive for the salvation of his soul, because he had been Superior for the space of twenty years, and I always fear much for those who are charged with the care of souls. Much grieved, I went to an oratory; there I conjured our Divine Lord to apply to this religious the little good I had done during my life, and to supply the rest by His infinite merits, in order that this soul might be freed from Purgatory.

Whilst I besought this grace with all the fervor of which I was capable, I saw on my right side this soul come forth from the depths of the earth and ascend into Heaven in transports of joy. Although this priest was advanced in years, he appeared to me with the features of man who had not yet attained the age of thirty, and with a countenance resplendent with light.

This vision, though very short, left me inundated with joy, and without a shadow of doubt as to the truth of what I had seen. As I was separated by a great distance from the place where this servant of God had ended his days, it was some time before I learned the particulars of his edifying death; all those who were witnesses of it could not behold without admiration how he preserved consciousness to the last moment, the tears he shed, and the sentiments of humility with which he surrendered his soul to God.

A religious of my community, a great servant of God, had been dead not quite two days. We were saying the Office for the Dead for her in choir, a sister was reading a lesson, and I was standing to say the versicle. When half of the lesson had been said, I saw the soul of this religious come forth from the depths of the earth, like the one of which I have just spoken, and go to Heaven.

In this same monastery there died, at the age of eighteen or twenty years, another religious, a true model of fervor, regularity, and virtue. Her life had been but a tissue of maladies and sufferings patiently endured. I had no doubt, after having seen her live thus, that she had more than sufficient merits to exempt her from Purgatory. Nevertheless, whilst I was at Office, before she was interred, and about a quarter of an hour after her death, I saw her soul likewise issue from the earth and rise to Heaven.

St. Louis Bertrand

St. Louis Bertrand, a Dominican, reported a similar story about Purgatory. In the year 1557, while St. Louis Bertrand lived at the convent of Valentia, a plague broke out in the city. The disease spread rapidly, threatening to kill many of the citizens. A priest, wishing to prepare himself for death, made a general confession of his whole life to the saint; and on leaving he said, "Father, if it should now please God to call me, I shall return and make known to you my condition in the other life."

The man died a little while afterwards, and the following night he appeared to the saint. He told St. Bertrand that he reportedly was detained in Purgatory on account of a few slight faults which remained to be expiated, and pleaded that St. Bertrand recommend his intentions to the community. St. Louis communicated the request immediately to his superior, who quickly recommend the soul to the prayers and the Holy Sacrifices of the community.

Six days later, a man who knew nothing of what had occurred at the convent, came to make his confession to Father Louis. He then told him, "the soul of Father Clement" had appeared to him. He saw, he said, the earth open, and the soul of the deceased priest come forth all glorious; it resembled, he said, a resplendent star, "which rose through the air towards Heaven."

St. Magdalen de Pazzi

St. Magdalen de Pazzi was also witness to the deliverance of a soul from Purgatory. One of her sisters had died, and the saint, praying one day before the Blessed Sacrament, saw her soul rise from the earth, still held in Purgatory. The sister was surrounded with flames under which a robe of brilliant whiteness protected her from the heat of the fire; she remained an entire hour at the foot of the altar, also adoring the Blessed Sacrament. This hour of adoration, which Magdalen saw the deceased sister perform, was the last of her penance in Purgatory.

St. Magdalen De Pazzi also said she witnessed a vision where different prisons of Purgatory were shown to her. In one she saw the soul of her brother, who had died after having led a good life. Still, his soul was detained in Purgatory for certain faults, that it had not sufficiently expiated in life. Struck with this vision, she went to her superior and reportedly said," "O my dear Mother, how terrible are the pangs of Purgatory! Never could I have believed it, had not God manifested it to me.... And, nevertheless, I cannot call them cruel; rather are they advantageous, since they lead to the ineffable bliss of Paradise."

Blessed Stephanie Quinziani

Blessed Stephanie Quinziani was a Dominican nun who wrote of a fellow sister named Paula who had died at the convent of Mantua after a long life of virtue. After her death, Sister Paula appeared, asking Blessed Stephanie for assistance with her suffering in Purgatory:

> Help me, dear sister, succor me in the frightful torture which I endure. Oh! If you knew the severity of the Judge who desires all our love, what atonement He demands for the least faults before admitting us to the reward! If you knew how pure we must be to see the face of God! Pray! Pray, and do penance for me, who can no longer help myself.

Blessed Stephanie, moved by the prayer of the nun, took it upon herself to offer prayers, penances, and good work. She eventually learned that Sister Paula was delivered from Purgatory.

Blessed Margaret Mary

Blessed Margaret Mary wrote of a dream in which she saw a soul that was held in Purgatory. This soul reportedly suffered for her unkind words and certain evil sentiments in her lifetime:

I saw in a dream, one of our sisters who had died some time previous. She told me that she suffered much in Purgatory, but that God had inflicted upon her a suffering which surpassed all other pains, by showing her one of her near relatives precipitated into Hell.

At these words I awoke, and felt as though my body was bruised from head to foot, so that it was with difficulty I could move. As we should not believe in dreams, I paid little attention to this one, but the Religious obliged me to do so in spite of myself. From that moment she gave me no rest, and said to me incessantly, 'Pray to God for me; offer to Him your sufferings united to those of Jesus Christ, to alleviate mine; and give me all you shall do until the first Friday in May, when you will please communicate for me.' This I did, with permission of my superior.

Meanwhile the pain which this suffering soul caused me increased to such a degree that I could find neither comfort nor repose. Obedience obliged me to seek a little rest upon my bed; but scarcely had I retired when she seemed to approach me, saying, 'You recline at your ease upon your bed; look at the one upon which I lie, and where I endure intolerable sufferings.' I saw that bed, and the very thought of it makes me shudder. The top and bottom was of sharp flaming points which pierced the flesh. She told me then that this was on account of her sloth and negligence in the observation of the rules. 'My heart is torn.' she continued, 'and causes me the most terrible sufferings for my thoughts of disapproval and criticism of my superiors. My tongue is devoured by vermin, and, as it were, torn from my mouth continually, for the words I spoke against charity and my little regard for the rule of silence. Ah! Would that all souls consecrated to God could see me in these torments. If I could show them what is prepared for those who live negligently in their vocation, their zeal and fervor would be entirely renewed, and they would avoid those faults which now cause me to suffer so much.'

At this sight I melted into tears. 'Alas!' said the
soul, 'one day passed by the whole community in exact
observance would heal my parched mouth; another
passed in the practice of holy charity would cure my
tongue; and a third passed without any murmuring or
disapproval of superiors would heal my bruised heart;
but no one thinks to relieve me.'

After I had offered the Communion which she
had asked of me, she said that her dreadful torments were
much diminished, but she had still to remain a long time
in Purgatory, condemned to suffer the pains due to those
souls that have been tepid in the service of God. As for
myself," adds Blessed Margaret Mary, "I found that I
was freed from my sufferings, which I had been told
would not diminish until the soul herself should be
relieved.

St. Robert Bellarmine

St. Robert Bellarmine, a Doctor of the Church, wrote
extensively on Purgatory. He particularly addressed the duration of
time in Purgatory:

There is no doubt that the pains of Purgatory are not
limited to ten and twenty years, and that they last in
some cases entire centuries. But allowing it to be true
that their duration did not exceed ten or twenty years,
can we account it as nothing to have to endure for ten
or twenty years, the most excruciating sufferings
without the least alleviation? If a man was assured that
he should suffer some violent pain in his feet, or his head,
or teeth for the space of twenty years, and that without
ever sleeping or taking the least repose, would he not a
thousand times rather die than live in such a state? And
if the choice were given to him between a life thus
miserable and the loss of all his temporal goods, would
he hesitate to make the sacrifice of his fortune to be

delivered from such a torment? Shall we then find any difficulty in embracing labor and penance to free ourselves from the sufferings of Purgatory? Shall we fear to practice the most painful exercises: vigils, fasts, almsgiving, long prayers, and especially contribution, accompanied with sighs and tears?

St. Vincent Ferrer

St. Vincent Ferrer, a Dominican, had a sister who lived a very social active life. She was full of the spirit of this world, its pleasures, and was headed towards damnation. However, St. Vincent prayed for her conversion and his prayer was eventually answered. His sister fell sick; and, at the moment of death, confessed her sins with sincere repentance.

Some days after her death, while St. Vincent was celebrating a Mass, his sister appeared to him in the midst of flames. She reportedly said, "My dear brother, I am condemned to undergo these torments until the day of the Last Judgment. Nevertheless, you can assist me. The efficacy of the Holy Sacrifice is so great: offer for me about thirty Masses, and I may hope the happiest result." The saint agreed to her request. He celebrated the thirty Masses. And on the thirteenth day his sister again appeared to him surrounded by angels and was escorted to Heaven. Thanks to the Masses, an expiation of several centuries was reduced to thirty days.

St. Lidwina

St. Lidwina reportedly was permitted to see a soul in Purgatory who had received a long sentence. Fr. F. X. Schouppe, S.J., gives us this account from his book, *Purgatory*:

St. Lidwina saw in Purgatory a soul that suffered also for mortal sins not sufficiently expiated on earth. The incident is thus related in the life of the saint. A man who had been for a long time a slave of the demon of impurity, finally had the happiness of being converted. He confessed his sins with great contrition, but, prevented by death, he had not time to atone by just penance for his numerous sins. Lidwina, who knew him well, prayed much for him. Twelve years after his death she still continued to pray, when, in one of her ecstasies, being taken into Purgatory by her angel guardian, she heard a mournful voice issuing from a deep pit. "It is the soul of that man," said the angel, "for whom you have prayed with so much fervor and constancy." She was astonished to find him so deep in Purgatory twelve years after his death.

The angel, seeing her so greatly affected, asked if she was willing to suffer something for his deliverance. "With all my heart," replied the charitable maiden. From that moment she suffered new pains and frightful torments, which appeared to surpass the strength of human endurance. Nevertheless, she bore them with courage, sustained by a charity stronger than death, until it pleased God to send her relief. She then breathed as one restored to a new life, and, at the same time, she saw that soul for which she had suffered so much come forth from the abyss as white as snow and take its flight to Heaven.

St. Bridget

The revelations of St. Bridget of Sweden include her experiences with the souls in Purgatory. Fr. Schouppe discusses these experiences, as well as her visits to Purgatory:

Souls that allow themselves to be dazzled by the vanities of the world, even if they have the good fortune to escape damnation, will have to undergo terrible punishment. Let us open the *Revelations of St. Bridget*, which are held in such esteem by the Church. We read there in Book Six that the saint saw herself transported in spirit into Purgatory, and that, among others, she saw there a young lady of high birth who had formerly abandoned herself to the luxury and vanities of the world. This unfortunate soul related to her the history of her life, and the sad state in which she then was.

"Happily," said she, "before death I confessed my sins in such dispositions as to escape Hell, but now I suffer here to expiate the worldly life that my mother did not prevent me from leading! Alas!" she added, with a sigh, "this head, which loved to be adorned, and which sought to draw the attention of others, is now devoured with flames within and without, and these flames are so violent that every moment it seems to me that I must die. These shoulders, these arms, which I loved to see admired, are cruelly bound in chains of red-hot iron. These feet, formerly trained for the dance, are now surrounded with vipers that tear them with their fangs and soil them with their filthy slime; all the members which I have adorned with jewels, flowers, and other ornaments, are now a prey to the most horrible torture."

"O mother, mother!" she cried, "how culpable have you been in my regard! It was you who, by a fatal indulgence, encouraged my taste for display and extravagant expense; it was you that took me to assemblies which are the ruin of souls....If I have not incurred eternal damnation, it was because a special grace of God's mercy touched my heart with sincere repentance. I made a good confession, and thus I have been delivered from Hell, yet only to see myself precipitated into the most horrible torments of Purgatory." We have remarked already that what is said of the tortured members must not be taken literally, because the soul is separated from the body; but God, supplying the want of corporal organs, makes the soul experience such sensations as have just been described. The biographer of the saint tells us that she related this vision to a cousin of the deceased, who was likewise given to the illusions of worldly vanity. The cousin was so struck that she renounced the luxuries and dangerous amusements of the world, and devoted the remainder of her life to penance in an austere religious order.

The same St. Bridget, during another ecstasy, beheld the judgment of a soldier who had just died. He had lived in the vices too common in his profession, and would have been condemned to Hell had not the Blessed Virgin, whom he had always honored, preserved him from the misfortune by obtaining for him the grace of a sincere repentance. The saint saw him appear before the judgment seat of God and condemned to a long Purgatory for the sins of all kinds which he had committed. "The punishment of the eyes," said the Judge, "shall be to contemplate the most frightful objects; that of the tongue, to be pierced with pointed needles and tormented with thirst; that of the touch, to be plunged in an ocean of fire." Then the Holy Virgin interceded, and obtained some mitigation of the rigor of the sentence.

St. Catherine of Siena

St. Catherine of Siena, a Doctor of the Church, asked God to please allow her to take on the suffering due her father in Purgatory. Fr. Schouppe relays the description of this ordeal by her biographer, Blessed Raymond of Capua:

The life of Jacomo finally approached its end and he was confined to bed by a dangerous illness. Seeing his condition, his daughter, as was her custom, betook herself to prayer, beseeching her Heavenly Spouse to save him whom she so tenderly loved. He answered that Jacomo was at the point of death, and that to live longer would not be profitable to him. Catherine then went to her father, and found him so perfectly resigned to leave this world, and without any regret, that she thanked God with all her heart.

But her filial love was not content; she returned to prayer in order to obtain from God, the Source of all grace, to grant her father not only the pardon of all his faults, but also that at the hour of his death he might be admitted into Heaven, without so much as passing through the flames of Purgatory. She was answered that justice could not sacrifice its rights; that the soul must be perfectly pure to enter the glory of Paradise. "Your father," said our Lord, "has led a good life in the married state, and has done much that was very pleasing in My sight; above all, his conduct towards you has been most agreeable to Me; but My justice demands that his soul should pass through fire, in order to purify it from the stains which it contracted in the world."

"O my loving Saviour," replied Catherine, "how can I bear the thought of seeing him who has nourished me, who has brought me up with such tender care, who has been so good to me during his whole life, tormented in those cruel flames? I beseech Your Infinite Goodness not to permit his soul to leave his body until in some way or another it shall have been so perfectly cleansed that it shall have no need to pass through the fires of Purgatory."

Admirable condescension! God yielded to the prayer and desire of His creature. The strength of Jacomo was exhausted, but his soul could not depart as long as the conflict lasted between our Lord, who alleged His Justice, and Catherine, who implored His Mercy. Finally, Catherine requested: "If I cannot obtain this grace without satisfying Thy justice, let, then, that justice be exercised upon me; I am ready to suffer for my father all that thy goodness may be pleased to send me." Our Lord consented. "I will accept thy proposal," He said, "on account of thy love for Me. I exempt thy father's soul from all expiation, but thou shalt suffer as long as thou livest the pain that was designed for him." Full of joy, Catherine cried out, "thanks for Thy word, O Lord, and may Thy will be done!"

The saint immediately returned to her father, who had just entered upon his agony. She filled him with courage and joy by giving him, on the part of God, the assurance of his eternal salvation, and she left him not until he had breathed forth his soul.

At the same moment that the soul of her father was separated from the body, Catherine was seized with most violent pains, which remained until her death, without allowing her one moment of repose. She herself often assured me of this, and indeed it was evident to all who saw her. But her patience was greater than her malady. All that I have related I learned from Catherine, when, touched at the sight of her sufferings, I asked her the cause thereof. I must not forget to say that at the moment her father expired she was heard to cry out, her face beaming with joy and a smile upon her lips, "May God be praised! My dear father, how I wish I were like you." During the celebration of the funeral...when all were in tears, Catherine seemed transported with delight. She consoled her mother and everyone as though unaffected by her father's death. It was because she had seen that beloved soul come forth triumphant from the prison of the body and pass without any hindrance into eternal beatitude. This sight had inundated her with consolation, because a short time previous she herself had tasted the joys of eternal light.

Let us here admire the wisdom of Providence. The soul of Jacomo could surely have been purified in another manner, and have been immediately admitted into Heaven, like the good thief who confessed our Saviour on the cross. But God willed that his purification should be effected through the sufferings of Catherine, as she herself had requested, and this not to try her, but to increase her merits and her crown.

It was fitting that his holy maid, who so ardently loved the soul of her father, should receive some recompense for her filial affection; and since she had preferred the salvation of his soul to that of her own body, her bodily suffering contributed to the happiness of her soul. Thus she always spoke of her sweet, her dear sufferings. And she was right, for the afflictions augmented the sweetness of grace in this life and the delights of glory in the next. She confined to me that long after his death her father Jacomo continually came to thank her for the happiness has had procured for him. He revealed many hidden things to her, warned her of the snares of the demon, and preserved her from all danger.

St. Peter Damien

St. Peter Damien wrote that each year, on the Feast of the Virgin Mary's Assumption into Heaven, thousands of souls are released from Purgatory through her intervention. St. Peter Damien reportedly conveyed the account of a miraculous vision regarding this annual event:

It is a pious custom, he says, which exists among the people of Rome to visit the churches, carrying a candle in the hand, during the night preceding the Feast of the Assumption of Our Lady. Now it happened that a person of rank, being on her knees in the basilica of the Ara-Coeli in the Capitol, saw before her, prostrate in prayer, another lady, her godmother, who had died several months previous. Surprised, and not being able to believe her eyes, she wished to solve the mystery, and for his purpose placed herself near the door of the church.

As soon as she saw the lady go out, she took her by the hand and drew her aside. "Are you not," she said to her, "my godmother, who held me at the baptismal font?" "Yes," replied the apparition immediately, "it is I." "And how comes it that I find you among the living, since you have been dead more than a year?" "Until this day I have been plunged in a dreadful fire, on account of many sins of vanity which I committed in my youth, but during this great solemnity the Queen of Heaven descended into the midst of the Purgatorial flames and delivered me, together with a large number of other souls, that we might enter Heaven on the Feast of her Assumption. She exercises this great act of clemency each year; and, on this occasion alone, the number of those whom she has delivered equals the population of Rome."

The apparition added, "In proof of the truth of my words, know that you yourself will die a year hence, on the feast of the Assumption; if you outlive that period, believe that this was an illusion."

Indeed, the feast of the Assumption is a great day of mercy towards the poor souls, Mary delights to introduce her children into the glory of Heaven on the anniversary of the day on which she herself first entered into Heaven. This belief, is founded on a great number of particular revelations; and it is for this reason that in Rome the Church of St. Mary in Montorio, which is the center of the archconfraternity of *suffrages for the dead*, is dedicated under the title of the Assumption.

As already demonstrated from the excerpts in this writing, perhaps no book on Purgatory brings this Catholic teaching to life as Fr. Schouppe's book, *Purgatory, As Explained By the Lives and Legends of the Saints*. The following accounts are also excerpted from this exceptional work:

The Location of Purgatory

It has pleased God to show in spirit the gloomy abodes of Purgatory to some privileged souls, who were to reveal the sorrowful mysteries thereof for the edification of the faithful.. Of this number was the illustrious St. Frances, foundress of the Oblates, who died in Rome in 1440. God favored her with great lights concerning the state of souls in the other life. She saw Hell and its horrible torments; she saw also the interior of Purgatory, and the mysterious order—I had almost said hierarchy of expiation—which reigns in this portion of the Church of Jesus Christ.

In obedience to her superiors...she made known all that God had manifested to her; and her visions, written at the request of the venerable Canon Matteotti, her spiritual director....Now, the servant of God declared that, after having endured with unspeakable horror the vision of Hell, she came out of that abyss and was conducted by her celestial guide into the regions of Purgatory. There reigned neither horror nor disorder, nor despair nor eternal darkness; there divine hope diffused its light, and she was told that this place of purification was called also *sojourn of hope*. She saw there souls which suffered cruelly, but angels visited and assisted them in their sufferings.

Purgatory, she said, is divided into three distinct parts, which are as the three large provinces of that kingdom of suffering. They are situated the one beneath the other, and occupied by souls of different orders. These souls are buried more deeply in proportion as they are more defiled and farther removed from the time of their deliverance.

The lowest region is filled with a fierce fire, but which is not dark like that of Hell; it is a vast burning sea, throwing forth immense flames. Innumerable souls are plunged into its depths: they are those who have rendered themselves guilty of mortal sin, which they have duly confessed, but not sufficiently expiated during life. The servant of God then learned that, for all forgiven mortal sin, there remains to be undergone a suffering of seven years. This term cannot evidently be taken to mean a definite measure, since mortal sins differ in enormity, but as an average penalty. Although the souls are enveloped in the same flames, their sufferings are not the same; they differ according to the number and nature of their former sins.

In this lower purgatory the saint beheld laics and persons consecrated to God. The laics were those who, after a life of sin, had had the happiness of being sincerely converted; the persons consecrated to God were those who had not lived according to the sanctity of their state. At that same moment she saw descend the soul of a priest whom she knew, but whose name she does not reveal. She remarked that he had his face covered with a veil which concealed a stain. Although he had led an edifying life, this priest had not always observed strict temperance, and had sought too eagerly the satisfactions of the table.

The saint was then conducted into the intermediate Purgatory, destined for souls which had deserved less rigorous chastisement. It had three distinct compartments; one resembled an immense dungeon of ice, the cold of which was indescribably intense; the second, on the contrary, was like a huge cauldron of boiling oil and pitch; the third had the appearance of a pond of liquid metal resembling molten gold or silver.

The upper Purgatory, which the saint does not describe, is the temporary abode of souls which suffer little, except the pain of loss, and approach the happy moment of their deliverance. Such in substance, is the vision of St. Francis relative to Purgatory....

That which shows still more the rigor of Purgatory is that the shortest period of time there appears to be of very long duration. Everyone knows that days of enjoyment pass quickly and appear short, whilst the time passed in suffering we find very long. Oh, how slowly pass the hours of the night for the poor sick, who spend them in sleeplessness and pain. We may say that the more intense the pain the longer appears the shortest duration of time. This rule furnishes us with a new means of estimating the sufferings of Purgatory.

We find in *The Annals of the Friar Minors*, under the year 1285, a fact which is also related by St. Antonius in his *Summa*. (Part 4, 4). A religious man suffering for along time from a painful malady, allowed himself to be overcome by discouragement, and entreated God to permit him to die, that he might be released from his pains. He did not think that the prolongation of his sickness was a mercy of God, who wished to spare him more severe suffering. In answer to his prayer, God charged his angel guardian to offer him his choice, either to die immediately and submit to the pains of Purgatory for three days, or to bear his sickness for another year and then go directly to Heaven.

The sick man, having to choose between three days in Purgatory and one year of suffering upon earth, did not hesitate, but took the three days in Purgatory. After the lapse of an hour, his angel went to visit him in his sufferings. On seeing him, the poor patient complained that he had been left so long in those torments. "And yet," he added, "you promised that I should remain here but three days." "How long," asked the angel, "do you think you have already suffered?" "At least for several yeas," he replied, "and I had to suffer but three days." Know, said the angel, "that you have been here only one hour." The intensity of the pain deceives you as to the time; it makes an instant appear a day, and an hour years." "Alas! then," said he with a sigh, "I have been very blind and inconsiderate in the choice I have made. Pray God, my good angel, to pardon me...."

Chapter Six

PURGATORY TODAY

Contemporary private revelations have clearly contributed to our growing understanding of Purgatory. And many 20th century accounts of visions, revelations, and dreams involving Purgatory are still being recorded. Though nothing startlingly new has been revealed, the revelations clarify and illuminate existing Church teachings. They also help us to apprehend the "reality" of Purgatory—a reality as genuine as Heaven and Hell. The following excerpts provide a sampling of some of the most profound revelations of Purgatory from the 20th century.

Padre Pio

Francesco Forgione, known to the world as Padre Pio, is considered by many to be the greatest mystic of the 20th century. Known for his bloody stigmata, Padre Pio is on record as having been blessed with almost every mystical gift known to the Church. Not surprisingly, Padre Pio claimed a great relationship with the suffering souls of Purgatory and even requested permission of his spiritual director in 1910 to offer himself as a victim soul for the souls in Purgatory:

> Now, my dear father, I want to ask your permission for something. For some time I have felt the need to offer myself to the Lord as a victim for poor sinners and for the souls in Purgatory. The desire has been growing continually in my heart, so that it has now become what I would call a strong passion. I have, in fact, made this offering to the Lord several times,

beseeching Him to pour upon me the punishment prepared for sinners and for the souls in Purgatory, even increasing them a hundredfold for me, as long as He converts and saves sinners and quickly admits to Paradise the souls of Purgatory. But I should now like to make this offering to the Lord in obedience to you. It seems to me that Jesus really wants this. I am sure that you will have no difficulty in granting me this permission.[1]

Following are two accounts of Padre Pio's interactions with the suffering souls in Purgatory. They are excerpted from the highly recommended book *The Holy Souls, Viva Padre Pio* by Fr. Alessio Parente O.F.M.Cap. (National Centre for Padre Pio, Inc.):

FROM PURGATORY TO HEAVEN

It was the usual evening scene in the friary's refectory (dining room). The friars, as was customary, had come together to partake of their frugal meal, and Padre Pio, too, was nibbling at something. The lively chattering was abruptly cut off by a brusque movement on the part of Padre Pio. He suddenly darted to the door of the friary and started up a lively conversation with some people, who, however, remained invisible to the other friars who had followed him. As they watched Padre Pio talking to what seemed to them to be nobody, the friars remarked to one another: "He has gone crazy!" However, they asked him whom he was talking to. Understanding their chagrin, he smiled and answered: "Oh, don't worry. I was talking to some souls who were on their way from Purgatory to Heaven. They stopped here to thank me because I remembered them in my Mass this morning." With this, he returned to his place in the refectory as if nothing out of the ordinary had happened.

Indeed, as we know, nothing out of the ordinary had happened at all, for souls of the dead were frequent visitors to him during the fifty-two years he spent at San Giovanni Rotondo. From the testimonies of some of Padre Pio's spiritual children and from the facts reported in the friary's chronicles, it is obvious that his association with these supernatural beings was not imaginary but was a reality. These souls he saw not with his mind's eye but with his physical eyes.

During his early years at San Giovanni Rotondo, he was in charge of the young students for the priesthood. He often spoke to them of the pains and sufferings of the souls in Purgatory and of our duty to help them with our prayers, mortifications, and other meritorious works. To encourage prayers and good works for the Holy Souls, Padre Pio would often relate to the seminarians his own personal experiences with deceased souls, telling them that these souls came to him to seek his prayers.

Toward the end of 1937, Padre Bernardo D'Alpicella, Provincial at that time, passed away. As was the custom, all the priests of the Province celebrated three Masses for his soul. One night, around the time of Padre Bernardo's death, Padre Pio had just finished praying and was about to leave the choir loft for one or two hours rest. But before doing so he approached the railing of the balcony and looked intently at the tabernacle to greet Jesus affectionately before leaving Him in the company of the angels. While he was looking at the tabernacle, he saw—clearly and distinctly—the late Padre Bernardo walking from Our Lady's altar toward the sacristy. Padre Pio witnessed this for three consecutive nights, and many friars received confirmation of this from him. Padre Raffaele, Padre Pio's companion, commented: "Padre Bernardo may have appeared to Padre Pio to thank him for his prayers and to let him understand that more prayers were needed for the release of his soul from Purgatory."

FOR LACK OF DILIGENCE

One evening, while the friars were at supper in the refectory (this occurred around 1921 or 1922), Padre Pio was praying in the choir loft. Around that time Padre Pio didn't go to the refectory for supper, but he used to remain in the choir loft and join the other friars later on, to warm himself at the communal fireplace. Padre Pio heard a scratching noise coming from the church—from the side altars.

He pricked his ears to be sure that he wasn't imagining things. Suddenly another noise—the sound of candles and candelabra falling from the high part of the main altar—filled the silence. Padre Pio's first thought was that it was one of the students going about his business who had caused the candles to fall. To verify this, he leaned over the balcony of the choir loft to have a closer look. How surprised he was to see a young friar, on the epistle side of the altar, motionless.

"What are you doing there?" Padre Pio asked in a commanding manner. He received no reply. So he continued: "This is a nice way to do your chores! Instead of putting things in order, you break the candles and the candle holders!"
However, the silence of the friar was as that of the tomb. He continued to remain absolutely motionless. So Padre Pio said in a loud commanding voice: "You! What are you doing there?"

Then the little friar replied: "I am brother... from..." But Padre Pio insisted: What are doing there at this hour?"

The little friar replied: "I am doing my Purgatory here. I was a student in this friary, so I now have to make amends for the errors I committed while I was here, for my lack of diligence in doing my duty in this church."

Padre Pio said to him: "Well, listen! I will say Mass for you tomorrow, but you mustn't come here anymore."

With his heart beating faster than usual, Padre Pio left the choir loft and made his way to the communal fireplace, where he found his conferees. They immediately noticed his agitation and asked him the reason; but he avoided their enquiring looks and questions and said only that he felt cold.

Barely ten minutes passed when Padre Pio asked one of the friars to accompany him to the church. There, on the altar, they found candles and candlesticks overturned. Padre Pio wanted to assure himself that he had heard correctly and that his imagination had not played tricks on him.

When he spoke of this occurrence later on he usually concluded with this observation: "For lack of diligence in doing his duty, that friar was still in Purgatory sixty years after his death! Imagine, then how much longer and how much more difficult Purgatory will be for those who commit sins which are more serious.

Sr. Faustina Kowalska

The Polish visionary, mystic and victim soul, Sister Faustina Kowalska reported in her diary an experience involving Purgatory. Like her accounts of Heaven and Hell, they add unique, important insight into Purgatory, especially in the understanding of how God's mercy and justice are one:

> Once I was summoned to the judgment (seat) of God. I stood alone before the Lord. Jesus appeared such as we know Him during His Passion. After a moment, His wounds disappeared except for five, those in His hands, His feet and His side. Suddenly I saw the complete condition of my soul as God sees it. I could clearly see all that is displeasing to God. I did not know that even the smallest transgressions will have to be accounted for. What a moment! Who can describe it? To stand before

the Thrice-Holy God! Jesus asked me. **Who are You**? I answered, " I am Your servant, Lord." **You are guilty of one day of fire in purgatory**. I wanted to throw myself immediately into the flames of purgatory, but Jesus stopped me and said. **Which do you prefer, suffer now for one day in purgatory or for a short while on earth?** I replied, "Jesus, I want to suffer in purgatory, and I want to suffer also the greatest pains on earth, even if it were until the end of the world." Jesus said, **One** (of the two) **is enough; you will go back to earth, and there you will suffer much, but not for long; you will accomplish My will and My desires, and a faithful servant of Mine will help you to do this. Now rest your head on My bosom, on My heart, and draw from its strength and power for these sufferings, because you will find neither relief nor help nor comfort anywhere else. Know that you will have much, much to suffer, but don't let this frighten you; I am with you.** (*Diary 36*)

Father Stefano Gobbi

For over 25 years, Father Stefano Gobbi of Italy received messages from the Blessed Virgin. These revelations have covered almost every subject. The following message, "At the Hour of Your Death," deals specifically with the topic of Purgatory:

Beloved sons, today you are gathered together in prayer, as you call to mind your brothers who have gone before you in the sign of faith and are now sleeping the sleep of peace.

How great is the number of my beloved ones and children consecrated to my Immaculate Heart, who have now entered into the repose of the Lord!

Many of them are sharing in the fullness of joy, in the prefect possession of God and, together with the angelic cohorts, are lights which shine in the eternal blessedness of paradise.

Many are in purgatory, with the certainty of having been saved for ever, although still in the suffering of purification, because their possession of God is not yet full and perfect.

Today I want to tell you that these brothers of yours are especially close to you and form the most precious part of my victorious cohort. I have but one single cohort, just as my Church is one and one alone, united in the joyous experience of the communion of saints.

The saints intercede for you, light up your path, assist you with their most pure love, defend you from the subtle snares which my Adversary sets for you, and anxiously await the moment of your meeting.

The souls who are being purified pray for you, offer their sufferings for your well-being and, through your prayers, they are assisted in being set free from those human imperfections which prevent them from entering into the eternal joy of paradise.

Those saints who, while on earth, had lived the consecration to my Immaculate Heart, making up a crown of love to alleviate the sorrows of your heavenly Mother, form here above my most beautiful crown of glory. They are close to my throne and follow your heavenly Mother where ever she goes.

Those souls in purgatory who, while on earth, had formed part of my cohort, now enjoy a special union with me, feel in a special way my presence which sweetens the bitterness of their suffering, and shortens the time of their purifications. And it is I myself who go to receive these souls into my arms, that I may lead them into the incomparable light of paradise.

Thus, I am always close to all of you, my beloved ones and children consecrated to my Heart, during your painful earthly pilgrimage, but I am close to you in a most special way at the hour of your death.

How many times, as you recite the holy rosary,

have you repeated this prayer to me: "Holy Mary,
Mother of God, pray for us sinners, now and at the hour
of our death!" This is an invocation which I listen to
with great joy, and it is always heard by me. If, as
Mother, I am close to each one of my children at the
hour of death, I am especially close to you who, through
your consecration, have always lived in the secure
refuge of my Immaculate Heart.

At the hour of your death, I am close to you,
with the splendor of my glorified body, I receive your
souls into my motherly arms and I bring them before my
Son Jesus, for his particular judgment.

Think of how joyful must be the meeting of
Jesus with those souls who are presented to Him by his
very own Mother. This is because I cover them with
my beauty, I give them the perfume of my holiness, the
innocence of my purity, the white robe of my charity
and, where there remains some stain, I run my motherly
hand over it to wipe it away and to give you that
brightness which makes it possible for you to enter into
the eternal happiness of paradise.

Blessed are those who die close to your
heavenly Mother. Yes, blessed, because they die in the
Lord, they will find rest from their labors, and their good
deeds will follow them.

My beloved ones and children consecrated to
my Immaculate Heart, today I invite you to enter into
a great intimacy with me during your life, if you wish to
experience the great joy of seeing me close to you and
of welcoming your souls into my motherly arms, at the
hour of your death.[3]

Christina Gallagher

Christina Gallagher is a 46 year old Irish mystic who first started
to report mystical experiences in the mid–1980's. Like Padre Pio, she
is today a world famous stigmatist who has reported apparitions, visions,
locutions and many other incredible experiences, including visitations

to Purgatory. Here is an account of those experiences as excerpted from the author's book, *The Sorrow, The Sacrifice and the Triumph: The Visions, Apparitions, and Prophecies of Christina Gallagher.*

Around the same time Christina was shown Hell, she was also shown Purgatory and its suffering inhabitants. It was another dire sight. For some of these poor souls were also experiencing the affects of fire. Only this fire was the fire of purification, not damnation.

Again, the reality of purgatory shocked Christina. Like most people, it was not something she contemplated. Today, there is little mention of Purgatory, even among Catholics. It is, however, a teaching handed down from the apostles and found in sacred Scripture.

Purgatory is said to be a necessary part of the Justice of God, which responds to all sin. The Church teaches that the least sin displeases God. Thus, His Mercy which pardons, contains His Justice which cleanses.

Purgatory, therefore, is a place of justice. Many saints have witnessed and written about this transitory state. It is a frightening place, yet unlike Hell, it contains peace and hope.

In Purgatory, as in Hell, there is a double pain— the pain of loss and the pain of the senses. The pain of loss consists of being temporarily deprived of the sight of God, Who is the Supreme Good, the beatific end for which our souls are made. This is a moral thirst which torments the soul's love for God. While the pain of senses is similar to what we experience in our flesh.

Although its nature is not defined by faith, the doctors of the church believe this world of suffering is in a foggy, misty place of darkness, a vast area said to be ash gray and cloudy with different levels, some fiery. And from what Christina witnessed, Purgatory was just that.

The Irish visionary saw three levels of Purgatory. In each of them, she witnessed souls imprisoned. She especially shuddered at seeing a lower level of Purgatory, a place she was told was not the lowest. The lowest was called the Chamber of Suffering. It is a place written of on the pages of old Catholic history books detailing private revelation. And it is described as a frightful sight.

Saint Lydwine of Schiedam, who died in 1433, wrote of such a chamber from her own experiences in ecstasy. Upon seeing this lowest level of Purgatory, Saint Lydwine saw what appeared to be walled pits in an immense prison of fire. She inquired of her guide, an angel, "Is this then Hell, my brother?"

"No, sister," replied the angel, "but this part of Purgatory is bordering on Hell."

Another of Christina's experiences of Purgatory was being taken through a dismal passageway with a series of doorways on either side leading at the end to a wider door space from which Christina's soul recoiled but towards which she was relentlessly impelled. Christina had to stop at each doorway where she experienced the inner agonies being endured by the various souls in these different caverns. The final one was the most horrific. Yet as soon as she surrendered to go there she was instantly consumed in a ball of light.

Like other witnesses to Purgatory, Christina remembers it as a dismal place of "gray ashes and little light," with all types of people, even priests, in great distress. Those she saw were in constant torment and hungered to see God. They even emitted a horrid smell. Christina said, "It was horrible. Really, really horrible."

Like earthly prisoners, the souls in Purgatory longed to be released from their sadness, captivity and suffering. They wanted out. And when these souls saw Christina they immediately begged her for help.

From his notes, Christina's spiritual director reports the Irish seer has been visited by many souls from Purgatory—priests, laity, even Bishops—all asking for her prayers, all wanting to be released.

On November 2, 1992, Christina received a vision that described the plight of those in Purgatory. "The souls in Purgatory. I can see them in a sea of gray cloud, reaching up to me and calling me by name saying, 'Christina, pray for me, pray for me,' and reaching up for my Rosary beads." And on December 4, 1993, she again saw them pleading for help with hands stretched out. Christina said it reminded her of the way people in Saint Peter's Square in Rome reach out to touch the Holy Father.

On another occasion, she was taken by Jesus through a narrow path, down some steps into a dark tunnel that led to Purgatory. After a while, she came to some gates that opened as if by remote control. Here, she saw many people dressed in brown-colored garments with hoods on their heads; two of whom she immediately recognized. These poor souls had their heads flexed downward as if in agony.

Says Christina, "The ground was mucky looking, sort of muddy and smelly. I could feel a particular agony and sadness for those souls. I didn't know these people in the *s*ense of having a relationship with them or of knowing them personally. But I knew them to see. A priest and a lay person. They didn't get very near us. But, at the moment when I was there, it was just like I felt as if they were my own mother or my own father. I loved them so much. All of a sudden, Jesus left me. I was then trapped against what looked like a wall. It's hard to describe. I couldn't move, but I didn't mind. I just kept crying out, 'Jesus please release those two souls and if it's your will, let me stay here, but release those two souls.' During this experience, I had resigned myself to wait there; to go through whatever I had to go through in suffering. I saw demons playing with fire which they took in their paws and which they threw towards me in my helpless state. It was more painful than when earthly fire burns the flesh. Yet my longing for those two souls to be released was beyond anything I could understand. Then after this, an enormous ball of white light came and I was taken into it. Then it was all over."

Afterward, the Lord confirmed to her the two souls—the priest and the lay person—were indeed released. In late October 1993, at the House of Prayer, many souls from different levels of Purgatory again appeared and pleaded with Christina for her prayers and sufferings. One of them, a soul of English descent, spoke to Christina about the "faith of England and said it would be raised up through Jesus and in union with His Holy Mother, "Mediatrix of All Graces.""

From all of this, Christina has learned the great value of our intercession for the release of souls from Purgatory and of the role the House of Prayer is to have in God's plan for the souls in purgatory. For souls will do anything, says Christina, to be freed from their captivity, their suffering.

Indeed, St. Catherine of Siena, in order to spare her father the pains of Purgatory, even offered herself to Divine Justice to suffer in his place. Not surprisingly, God accepted her offer. It is said that from this Saint Catherine suffered excruciating torments the rest of her life till death, but her father was set free.

Like Saint Catherine, we are also in a position to help release souls. Especially by prayers, lots of prayers. "For our prayers," says Christina, "are the keys to their freedom."

Medjugorje

Since 1981, the Blessed Virgin Mary has been reportedly appearing to six individuals from Medjugorje, Hercegovina. Three of the visionaries still claim to be receiving apparitions (as of March 2000). Besides receiving numerous messages, the six visionaries at Medjugorje claim to have either visited or been shown Purgatory by the Blessed Mother.

Mirjana Dravicevic Soldo the oldest visionary at Medjugorje, said that there were several levels in Purgatory and that the more you pray while you are alive, the higher will be your level (if at all) of Purgatory. Mirjana said she did not know how long people stayed there, but did emphasize how Mary asked for prayers for the souls in Purgatory and how souls were helpless to pray for themselves. Christmas Day, said Mirjana, was when the most souls were released from Purgatory. Janice T. Connell, in her book *The Visions of the Children*, interviewed Mirjana about Purgatory:

Q.   Have you ever truly seen Purgatory?

A.   *Yes.*

Q.   Is it a place?

A.   *Yes.*

Q.   Is it geographically part of the planet earth, or is it somewhere else?

A.   *I saw one place. Many people were there. They were suffering immensely.*

Q.   What kind of suffering?

A.   *It was physical suffering?*

Q.   Where is this place?

A.   *I don't know.*

Q.   What kind of people were there? Old, young, fat, thin?

A.   *They were normal people, all kinds. There was much physical suffering.*

Q.   Can you describe the suffering you saw? Was it like leprosy of something similar to that?

A.   *I could see the people shivering, thrashing, and writhing in pain.*

Q.   Were the people cold? Was the place cold?

A.   *I saw this place for a short time. I didn't personally experience the temperature. The Blessed Mother was with me. She explained to me that she wanted me to see purgatory. She said so many people on earth today do not even know about purgatory.*

Q.   Have many people today forgotten about the justice of God?

A.   *Since nothing can live in the sight of God but pure love, God's justice cleanses. That's why we have purgatory.*

Q.   Mirjana, are you saying purgatory is an instrument of God's justice? We have been taught that God's justice is not like man's justice, for God has no cruelty. Cruelty is an attribute of pride.

A.   *The Blessed Mother has said God is pure love.*

Q.   Were the people in Purgatory screaming?

A.   *I could not hear them. I only saw them.*

Q.   Why did the Blessed Mother want to show you purgatory?

A.   *She said so many people who die are quite abandoned by their loved ones. They cannot help themselves in purgatory. They are totally dependent on the prayers and sacrifices of the generous people on earth who remember them. Our Blessed Mother hopes her own children will help the souls in purgatory by prayer and fasting and various penances for the poor souls to make restitution for them.*

Q.   Mirjana, why do people of the earth have to make restitution for people who have died?

A.   *Because those who have died no longer have free will as they had on earth. They no longer have a body. It's no longer possible for them to make up for the things that they did when they had their body that hurt and harmed themselves and others. Only July 24, 1982, the Blessed Mother said: "We go to heaven in full conscience: that which we have now. At the moment of death, we are conscious of the separation of the body and soul. It is false to teach people that we are reborn many times and that we pass to different bodies. One is born only once. The body, drawn from the earth, decomposes after death. It never comes back to life again. Man receives a transfigured body. Whoever has done very much evil during his life can go straight to heaven if he confesses, is [truly] sorry for*

> *what he has done, and receives Communion at the end of his life."*

Q. The good thief who died next to Jesus was the first canonized saint, wasn't he, Mirjana?

A. *Jesus Himself promised him paradise that very day!*

Q. Mirjana, how do the prayers of those who are still on earth and the penances help those who have died?

A. *The Blessed Mother explained that the prayers and the penance of those on the earth soften hearts of stone, melt hearts of stone. When the hearts of stone of God's children are melted, great love is possible, even on this earth.*

Q. Mirjana, is it true or do you know whether the poor souls in purgatory can see us the earth?

A. *They can see their loved ones during those moments when we pray for them by name.*

Q. Ivan told me the Blessed Mother said they are very lonely and she herself goes there often to comfort them.

A. *We too can comfort them with our prayers and sacrifices.*

Q. Mirjana, do you pray for the souls in purgatory?

A. *Yes, I have given my life to the Blessed Mother for the sake of the unbelievers.*

Another of the visionaries, **Ivanka Ivankovic Elez**, also reported witnessing Purgatory. It was filled with "darkness," said Ivanka, and the people were there "as a result of their choices in life."

Vicka Ivankovic, who has reportedly written a book on Mary's life as dictated to her by the Virgin, said that she couldn't see people in Purgatory, only a misty, gray, fog, that looked like "ashes." But Vicka did sense people "moaning, weeping, trembling," in what seemed like "terrible suffering." Like Mirjana, Vicka spoke of the souls' desperate need for prayers. The souls in Purgatory, she said, can see "us on earth" when we pray for them.

The oldest male visionary, **Ivan Dragicevic**, emphasized that Mary told him the souls in Purgatory believed in God while on earth, "only occasionally." They had doubt that God existed and did not know how to pray, he said. And if no one prays for them, they "suffer even more."

The youngest visionary, **Jacov Colo**, said he was shown Purgatory but did not visit it as he did Heaven. It was a place where souls were purified, said Jacov. He also said the reason he was shown Purgatory was so that on seeing its reality he might be a more effective witness of life itself.

Finally, **Marija Pavlovic Lunetti**, the visionary who receives Mary's monthly message for the world, said that she too has seen Purgatory. In *Queen of the Cosmos*, Janice T. Connell asks about her experience:

> Q.   Would you tell us about Purgatory?
> A.   *Yes, Purgatory is a large place. It is foggy. It is ash gray. It is misty. You cannot see people there. It is as if they are immersed in deep clouds. You can feel that the people in the mist are traveling, hitting each other. They can pray for us but not for themselves. They are desperately in need of our prayers. The Blessed Mother asks us to pray for the poor souls in Purgatory, because during their life here, one moment they thought there was no God, then they recognized Him, then they went to Purgatory where they saw there is a God, and now they need our prayers. With our prayers we can send them to Heaven. The biggest suffering that souls in Purgatory have is that they see there is a God, but they did not accept Him here on earth. Now they long so much to come close to God. Now they suffer so intensely, because they recognize how much they have hurt God, how many chances they had on earth, and how many times they disregarded God.*

Epilogue

AIDING THE POOR SOULS

From the very beginning of the Church, belief in Purgatory has been associated with the need and duty to help suffering souls through prayer and sacrifice. Therefore, the very exercise of this charity should be addressed. Since every Christian is aided by the merits of other Christians, who together make up the Mystical Body of Christ, helping to deliver a soul from Purgatory has been an established teaching of the Church for centuries. By definition of their status, the Church declares that souls in Purgatory can do nothing for themselves. They can no longer gain merit or sin, receive the Sacraments, or profit from indulgences. While prayers from the Church militant are acceptable, they are abandoned to their own fate and must hope in God and their fellow members of the Mystical Body of Christ to hasten their entrance into Heaven.

Perhaps in no greater way do the members of the Mystical Body of Christ—the Church—cooperate with each other. Through mutual joys and sufferings, the Church either triumphs together in Heaven, militates on earth, or suffers in Purgatory. By duty, we on earth must celebrate and rejoice over those who are in Heaven, console and aid our living brethren, and come to the assistance of the suffering souls in Purgatory. This is the Communion of the Saints—charity, mercy, consolation, and prayer. All of these work together, through grace, to unite the Body of Christ.

Relief and aid to the suffering souls in Purgatory has been addressed by the Church in such a formal and precise manner that Catholics can learn exactly what methods of assistance for the Suffering Souls in Purgatory are available to them. Historically, the Fathers of the Church divided the means of assisting the poor souls into three categories:

> 1) The Holy Sacrifice of the Mass
> 2) Prayer
> 3) Works of Expiation

The Holy Sacrifice of the Mass

According to theologians, the Sacrifice of the Mass has always been considered the most powerful and effective means of aiding and releasing souls in Purgatory. Beginning with a Catholic Burial, which includes the offering of a Mass for the deceased, no more profitable an act can be immediately instituted on behalf of the departed soul. St. Cyrillus instructed that "although we are sinners, we nevertheless send up our supplications to God for the departed, not offering Him, for instance a crown, but Jesus Christ Himself, who bled for our sins, and beseeching the bountiful and gracious God to be merciful to them and to us. We pray for all that have departed this life, because we confidently believe that the "prayer at the altar" will be most profitable to them."

Human acts, even prayers and almsgiving, are not as efficacious as a Mass offered by the great High priest, Jesus Christ Himself, to the Most Holy Trinity. In prayer, a creature intercedes for another creature, but in the Holy Mass, Christ intercedes. Because the Sacrifice is perfect, theologians tell us that it is the most efficient and speedy way in releasing souls from Purgatory.

In *Caring for the Suffering Souls*, Rev. John A. Nageleisen explains the importance of offering the Holy Sacrifice of the Mass for the deceased:

> As a Sacrifice of Propitiation, Holy Mass, therefore, has the power, and by the ordinance of Christ it is its object, infallibly and directly and in virtue of its own efficacy, to efface temporal punishment of sin. That this effect does not detract from the value of the sacrifice of the Cross, but that its infinite power and efficacy is rather emphasized thereby, is obvious to everyone having a true comprehension of Catholic doctrine. The Church does not teach that by the

sacrifice of Christ on the altar the treasure of redemption merited by His sacrifice on the cross is increased or receives new value, but that the unincreaseable and inexhaustible price of redemption paid for us through the sacrifice of the Cross is individually applied to us and made our own in Holy Mass. Christ's treasury of grace ever remains the same; but this grace is distributed and applied to the souls of men in Holy Mass. Consequently, the fruits of the Holy Sacrifice of Mass are in general the very same as those acquired by our Lord on the noble tree of the Cross. What was merited on the Cross for all mankind is intended to be made the property of the individual in Holy Mass; it is therefore a continual Sacrifice of Propitiation.

The Sacrifice of the Mass possesses an infinite efficacy which can neither be increased nor diminished by man, because Jesus Christ is at the same time the Minister and the Victim of the Sacrifice. For this reason it is a means of obtaining from God the most sublime gifts, in general and in particular. If Mass is celebrated for the Suffering Souls, there is no doubt that one Holy Sacrifice possesses of itself more power than is necessary to release at once all souls detained in Purgatory, as the Council of Trent teaches: "The fruits of the bloody sacrifice on the cross are distributed and received most profusely through the unbloody Sacrifice of the Mass."

Can we be astonished, when reflecting on the propitiatory powers of Holy Mass, that by it many souls are delivered at once from Purgatory? St. Nicholas of Tolentino saw a great number of Suffering Souls in a field, who all united in imploring him to celebrate Holy Mass for them. After having done so for eight days, it was revealed to him that the souls he had seen were all released. St. Anthony of Padua relates: Blessed John of Alverina once offered the Holy Sacrifice of the Mass on All Saints' Day. At the consecration, while holding the sacred Body of our Lord in his hands, he ardently implored the Heavenly Father, by the Blood and the merits of His only Son, to release the Souls from Purgatory; and behold! He saw a great number of these holy souls, like sparks of fire escaping from a furnace soaring up triumphantly to the heavenly kingdom.

It must also be noted that a Mass said for one soul not only has value for that soul but is profitable for many souls. According to Fr. Lagrange, St. Thomas Aquinas and his understudies noted the great, unlimited value a Mass said has for all the souls in Purgatory:

> Can suffrages offered for one soul be profitable also for others? His answer runs thus: By intention, they have a special value for the one. But, by reason of charity which cannot exclude anyone, they are more profitable to those who have the greater charity and are thus better disposed to receive greater consolation. Thus, as regards Holy Mass, we distinguish the special fruit, granted to the soul for whom the Mass is said, from the general fruit, in which all the faithful, however numerous, participate, each in the measure of his own disposition.
>
> St. Thomas asks a second question: Are suffrages offered for many souls together more profitable than if they were offered for one? His answer runs thus: By reason of the charity which inspires them, these suffrages are just as profitable for many as if they were offered for one. One Mass gives joy to ten thousand souls in purgatory as if they were but one. Nevertheless these same suffrages, considered as satisfaction, are more useful to those to whom they are applied singly.
>
> This at least was the thought of St. Thomas, when, as a young priest, he wrote his commentary on the *Fourth Book of Sentences*. But at the end of his life when he was composing the *Summa*, he says regarding the sacrifice of the Mass: "Although one sacrifice of Mass is in itself sufficient to satisfy for all suffering, nevertheless its value, both for those for whom it is offered and for those who offer, is measured by their devotion. This measure of devotion depends, in the

case of the poor soul, on the disposition they had at the moment of death."

Here the only limit assigned to the satisfactory power of the Mass is the devotion of those who offer and of those for whom it is offered. Thus, it is generally admitted that the parochial Mass in a large parish is just as profitable to each member, according to his devotion, as it would be for each member of a small parish.

The great Thomistic commentators—Cajetan, John of St. Thomas, Gonet, the Carmelites of Salamanca—insist on the infinite value of the Mass, by reason of the victim offered, of the chief priest who offers. One Mass said for many persons can be just as profitable to each, according to the measure of his devotion, as if it were offered for one alone. The sun illuminates ten thousand people as easily as if they were but one person.

The effect of a universal cause is limited only by the capacity of its subjects to receive the influence of that cause.

Thus, Mass on All Souls Day, which is said for all the souls in purgatory, has special value for forgotten souls, for whom no one now offers a special Mass.

Prayer

Prayer for the poor souls in Purgatory is an important, efficacious way of helping them to gain Heaven. Jesus said, "If you ask the Father anything in my name, He will give it to you" (John 16:23). In this promise, we take our hearts, filled with love for our departed ones, and we raise up in prayer the petitions of imploring the release of their souls from Purgatory.

Theologians note that there are also certain conditions to remember which aid such prayer:

1)   The person praying, ideally, should be in a state of grace in order to possess supernatural life, which, in the sight of God, is most efficacious;

2)   Prayer must be voluntary, proceeding from free
        will;

3)   To be most meritorious, prayer must be
        addressed to God from a supernatural motive for
        His greater glory.

It must be noted that God hears all prayer, even that of sinners. But He need not respond, except through His mercy. But prayer from a soul in grace moves God and is, as St. Augustine says, "a key to heaven."

According to the saints, God is well pleased with prayer for the suffering souls and is touched by it to respond in mercy. Writes St. Bernard: "I will invoke the Lord with mournful lamentations, I will beseech Him with continued sighing. I will remember the departed in my prayers, hoping that the Lord will cast a pitying glance on them, and will change their torments into rest, their distress into ineffable glory. By such means their time of punishment can be shortened, their pains and torments mitigated."

According to many saints, the Rosary is a most appropriate, helpful prayer to be recited for the departed. The Virgin Mary told St. Dominic that "the release of the souls in Purgatory is one of the chief effects of the Rosary." Indeed, according to Blessed Alan de la Roche, many departed souls have returned in apparitions to reveal that, except for the Mass, no prayer is as powerful for the release of souls from Purgatory as the Rosary. This is because the Queen of Heaven is considered to be such a powerful intercessor for her afflicted children in Purgatory.

Likewise, through the special promises attached to those who wear her Scapular, Mary is also able to obtain the speedy release of souls from Purgatory. Fr. John A. Nageleisen writes of this promise:

> The clients of this Mother...are indeed to be called
> happy, for she is their consolation and help not only in
> this world, but also in Purgatory. Besides promising that
> she would preserve from hell those who devoutly wear
> her holy habit, the scapular of Mount Carmel, she added
> a second privilege, namely that of speedy release from
> Purgatory. This latter promise was made about seventy

years after the introduction of the scapular. Mary deigned to appear to Pope John XII and recommended to his care the Order of Carmelites. Extending her maternal solitude even to the next world, she promised to assist the souls of the members in Purgatory, to console them and to release them as soon as possible, particularly on the Saturday following their decease.

The Pope published this privilege in a Bull dated March 3, 1322. The meaning of this promise is that Mary gives those who wear the holy scapular and fulfill the conditions prescribed, as much assurance of their eternal salvation as can be obtained during mortal life, at the same time declaring that if they are constant in her service and lead a Christian life, they shall also receive the grace of final perseverance.

Mary is solicitous for the Suffering Souls in Purgatory because she is the Mother of pure souls. St. Bernardine remarks, "In this prison of the spouses of Christ, she exercises, so to say, absolute sovereignty in mitigating their pains, and in delivering them from sad imprisonment." Hence Mary descends with truly maternal charity into Purgatory and eases its torments. St. Bonaventure applies to her words, "I have penetrated into the bottom of the deep" (Ecclus 24: 8.), and adds, in our Blessed Mother's name, "into the abyss of Purgatory, there to mitigate the pains of the Suffering Souls." St. Vincent Ferrer exclaims, "O how amiable and benevolent Mary shows herself to them that suffer in Purgatory; for through her they continually receive comfort and consolation." By her meditation the poor captives are released from their fiery prison.

St. Bernadine remarks, "To Mary was given the power, by her intercession and merits, to release the souls from Purgatory, particularly those that were foremost in their devotion to her." St. Bridget one night was addressed by the Blessed Virgin as follows: "I am the Mother also of the souls in Purgatory. Their torments are continually eased in some manner through my intercession. For it pleases the Lord to remit in this manner some of the punishments which are their due by justice."

St. Thomas and nearly all the holy Fathers teach that the Blessed Virgin Mary comes to the aid of the Suffering Souls. The Church also, in the Masses of *Requiem,* prays that God may grant eternal bliss to the deceased through the intercession of the Blessed Virgin and all the saints."

Of course, the Rosary and Scapular are not the only ways one can help the suffering souls in Purgatory. Any prayer offered for this intention is worthy. Here are several efficacious prayers said for the souls in Purgatory:

Eternal Father, I offer Thee the Most Precious Blood of Thy Divine Son, Jesus, in union with the Masses said throughout the world today, for all the holy Souls in Purgatory, for sinners everywhere, for sinners in the Universal Church, those in my own home and those within my family. Amen. (Jesus reportedly told St. Gertrude the Great that this prayer would release 1,000 souls from Purgatory each time it is said. The prayer was extended to include living sinners which would alleviate the indebtedness accrued to them during their lives.)

O God, Creator and Redeemer of all the faithful, grant to the souls of our departed loved ones, the remission of all their sins, that by means of our pious supplications, they may obtain the joys of heaven, which they have ever earnestly desired. We ask this through Christ our Lord. Amen.

Eternal rest grant unto them, O Lord; and let perpetual light shine upon them. May their souls and the souls of all the faithful departed through the mercy of God rest in peace. Amen.

Works of Expiation

There is no limit to what can be offered in the form of works of expiation for the souls in Purgatory. From one's daily work to special acts of sacrifice such as fasting, almsgiving, and pilgrimages, the Church teaches that such efforts designated to help the poor souls are welcomed by God.

In order to aid the suffering souls, all such works are offered to God to render satisfaction for the sins that offend him. We are, through our works, satisfying the demands of divine justice and atoning the penalty of sinful gratification wrongfully indulged. God then rewards these efforts by giving relief to the suffering souls.

Fr. John A. Nageleisen explains how good works may be properly applied in expiation for the souls in Purgatory:

> Those Christians who mercifully and compassionately come to the relief of these suffering, yet most worthy souls by performing for their benefit all kinds of good works, may rest assured that God is supremely pleased therewith; and He will permit such souls in their turn, when in Purgatory, to receive speedily the benefit of the good works performed for them by the members of the Church militant. This we know from many private revelations. Sister Frances of the Blessed Sacrament was often visited by souls bringing tidings of others that were not permitted to appear to her. One day a deceased Sister asked her for prayers for four others who were not permitted to leave Purgatory. Another soul, in 1870, even refused to answer questions concerning certain deceased persons, because God did not permit it.
>
> On the part of the faithful the following conditions must be observed in order that their suffrages for the Suffering Souls may be accepted by God:
>
> a)   They must have the intention of resigning the merits of their good works in favor of the Suffering Souls. The fruit accruing from our good works remains our property as long as we

do not cede it to some other person. Our intention may specify a particular soul to whom we desire to apply our suffrages. If the soul for which we supplicate is already in heaven or in hell, God will give the benefit of our intercession to some other soul according to the pleasure of His wisdom, mercy, and justice. If the works of suffrage are offered for the relief of the Suffering Souls in general, the satisfactory fruit thereof is divided among them all.

b)   The work performed must be one of atonement. All good works are such; but they are not all equally valuable as atonement. Their atoning value depends either on the disposition of the person performing them; or it may be inherent in the works themselves, as for instance Holy Mass, indulgences, and the prayers of the Church.

c)   According to the unanimous doctrine of all theologians, the good works, to be effective, must be performed in the state of grace. Nevertheless there is no doubt that the atoning effect of such good works as possess atoning power of themselves, are of benefit to the Suffering Souls even though they be performed in the state of sin; such works are for instance Holy Mass, the personal or local plenary indulgence of a privileged altar, the prayers and blessings of the Church.

The Suffering Souls receive no benefit of a good work performed in the state of sin, when the value of this work requires it to be performed in the state of grace. If in such a case the petition of a sinner is granted, this is not done because the work itself was worthy favor, but solely and purely as a result of God's mercy. But if the sinner acts as the minister of the Church, or in the name of one actually in the state of grace,

then the good work has the same value that it
would have if the one ordering it had done the
work himself. Thus teaches the Angelic
Doctor, St. Thomas.

St. Chrysostom reminds us: "Of what benefit is
your excessive weeping? Not tears, but good
works aid the deceased." Charity is inventive;
and, the Christian soul, the true follower of
Christ, is all charity. Mindful of the departed, he
therefore says, "I will make good the
deficiencies of the Suffering Souls."

There are other ways to aid the suffering souls. It is most
profitable, the Church teaches, to invoke the saints and the angels and
to ask for their intercession. Likewise, over the centuries, confraternities
have arisen, whose members offer in union their prayers and sacrifices for
the souls in Purgatory.

On a more personal level, the burning of candles, the use of Holy
Water and even offering one's Holy Communion are all ways to help
the suffering souls in Purgatory. The great 19th century mystic, Anna
Marie Taigi, relayed the following story of how, in offering her
Communion one day, she came to help a soul obtain its release from
Purgatory. Fr. Albert Bessieres, S.J., includes this story in his book,
Wife, Mother and Mystic: The Life of Blessed Anna Marie Taigi:

Anna Mary Taigi, a holy woman of Rome, was also
privileged often to see released souls, who came to
thank her. One day she intended to receive holy
Communion in the basilica of St. John Lateran, and to
offer it for a certain deceased person. During the first
Mass at which she assisted, and which was celebrated by
her confessor, she was suddenly attacked with a great
depression of spirit joined with severe bodily pains.
Nevertheless she continued in prayer and offered up her
illness in atonement to divine justice. Then Cardinal
Pedicini began his Mass. At the *Gloria* the saintly
woman was suddenly seized with the great supernatural
joy and consultation. Then a soul just released from

Purgatory appeared to her and said, *"I thank thee, my sister, for thy compassion. I will remember thee at the throne of God; for thanks to thy prayer I now go to enter heaven, where I shall be in bliss forever."*

INSIDE PURGATORY

CHAPTER ONE
PERFECTION THROUGH PURIFICATION

The quotations from the *Catechism of the Catholic Church* are from 1994 edition, pg. 269, published by Urbi Et Orbi Communications and available through Inside the Vatican. Fr. John Laux's quote is from his book, *Chief Truths of the Faith*, pg. 162 (TAN Books). Pope John Paul II reflection on Purgatory was delivered on August 4, 1999.

CHAPTER TWO
PURGATORY: A DOCTRINE FOUND IN SCRIPTURE

The quotation of Fr. John Laux is from his book *Chief Truths of the Faith*, TAN Books, pg. 163. Much of the early Christian history of Purgatory came from Fr. Garrigou Lagrange's book *Everlasting Life* (TAN Books). St. Augustine's quote is from his book *Confessions*. The *Catechism of the Council of Trent* is published by TAN Books. Once again, I used the 1994 *Catechism of the Catholic Church*, published by Urbi Et Orbi Communications.

CHAPTER THREE
THE PAINS OF PURGATORY

The quotation from Fr. Garrigou Lagrange is from his book, *Life Everlasting*, pgs. 167-169, (TAN Books). St. Catherine of Genoa's quote is from her *Treatise on Purgatory* (TAN Books). Fr. Lagrange's words on fire being the source of purification in Purgatory is from his book *Everlasting Life*, pg 174. Rev. John A. Nageleisen's quotation is from his book *Care for Suffering Souls,* pgs. 47–48, (TAN Books). St. Thomas Acquinas' quotations, as well and St. Augustine's, were both taken from Fr. Lagrange's book, *Everlasting Life.* Fr. Lagrange's quotation on the concept of time in Purgatory is from the same book, pg. 177.

CHAPTER FIVE
PURGATORY AND THE SOULS

St. Catherine of Genoa's quotation is from her *Treatise of Purgatory, pgs 325-328,* (TAN Books). St. Teresa of Avila's account of Purgatory is Fr. F.X. Schouppe's classic *Purgatory, Explained By the Lives and Legends of the Saints,* pgs. 11–14, (TAN Books). The accounts of Purgatory from St. Louis Bertrand, St. Magdalen de Pazzi, Blessed Stephanie Quiziani, Blessed Margaret Mary, St. Robert Bellarmine, St. Vincent Ferrer, St. Lidwina, St. Bridget, St. Catherine of Siena, and St. Peter Damien are all from Father Schouppe's book, which I highly recommend. Likewise, the information on the location of Purgatory is from this book.

CHAPTER SIX
PURGATORY TODAY

The two accounts of Padre Pio's experiences with Purgatory are from the book, *The Holy Souls, Viva Padre Pio* from The National Centre for Padre Pio. His letter to his spiritual director offering himself as a victim soul for the souls in Purgatory is also from this book. This book I highly recommend. (You can order it from the National Centre for Padre Pio Inc. 2213 Old Route 100, Barto, PA, 19504, USA). Saint Faustina Kowalska's account of Purgatory is from her book, *Divine Mercy in My Soul, The Diary of Sister M. Kowalska Faustina,* pg. 19. This book I also highly recommend and is available from Marian Press, Stockbridge, Mass.

The revelations of the Blessed Virgin Mary to Father Stefano Gobbi are from the book *To the Priests, Our Lady's Beloved Sons,* published by the Marian Movement of Priests. Christina Gallagher's account of Purgatory is from the author's book, *The Sorrow, the Sacrifice and the Triumph, The Apparitions, Visions and Prophecies of Christina*

Gallagher (Simon and Schuster).

The accounts of Purgatory from the visionaries at Medjugorje came primarily from Janice T. Connell's two excellent books, *Queen of the Cosmos* (Paraclete Press) and *The Visions of the Children* (St. Martins). I highly recommend both of these books.

EPILOGUE
AIDING THE POOR SOULS

The means sighted in this chapter for aiding the poor souls in Purgatory primarily comes from Rev. John Nageleisen's *Caring for the Suffering Souls* (TAN Books). He is quoted from this book throughout the chapter. Fr. Garrigou Lagrange's quotation is from his book, *Everlasting Life,* pgs. 198-199, (TAN Books).

SELECTED BIBLIOGRAPHY

Arnendzen, J.P., D.D. *Purgatory and Heaven.* TAN Books and Publishers, Inc., 1972.

Brown, Michael H. *Afterlife.* Milford, Ohio: Faith Publishing Company, 1997.

Carty, Rev. Charles Mortimer. *Padre Pio, The Stigmatist.* Rockford, Illinois: TAN Books and Publishers, Inc., 1973.

Carty, Fr. Chas. M. & Rev. Dr. David L. Rumble, M.S.C. *Purgatory Quizzess to a Street Preacher.* Rockford, Illinois: TAN Books and Publishers, Inc., 1976.

----. *Catechism of the Catholic Church.* New Hope, Kentucky: St. Martin de Porres Community, 1994.

Chervin, Ronda DeSola. *Quotable Saints.* Ann Arbor, Michigan: Servant Publications, 1992.

Connell, Janice T. *Queen of the Cosmos.* Orleans, Massachusetts: Paraclete Press, 1990.

Connell, Janice T. *The Visions of the Children.* New York: St. Martin's Press, 1992.

Gobbi, Don Stefano. *Our Lady Speaks to Her Beloved Priests.* St. Francis, Maine: National Headquarters of the Marian Movement of Priests in the United States of America, 1988.

Gobbi, Don Stefano. *To the Priests Our Lady's Beloved Sons*. St. Francis, Maine: National Headquarters of the Marian Movement of Priests in the United States of America, (Supplement, 1996).

Lagrange, Garrigou, Fr. Reginald, O.P. *Everlasting Life*. Rockford, Illinois: TAN Books and Publishers, Inc., 1991.

Laurentin, Rene and Ljudevit Rupcic. *Is the Virgin Mary Appearing at Medjugorje?* Washington, D.C.: The Word Among Us Press, 1984.

Laux, Fr. John, M.A. *Church History*. Rockford, Illinois: TAN Books and Publishers Inc., 1989.

Laux, Fr. John, M.A. *Chief Truths of the Faith. A Course in Religion Book I*. Rockford, Illinois: TAN Books and Publishers, Inc., 1990.

Lord, Bob & Penny, *Visions of Heaven Hell and Purgatory*. Robert and Penny Lord, 1996.

Liguori, St. Alphonsus, *Preparation for Death*. Rockford, Illinois: TAN Books and Publishers, Inc., 1982.

Manning, Henry Edward. *Sin and Its Consequences*. Rockford, Illinois: TAN Books and Publishers, Inc., 1986.

McDannell, Colleen & Bernhard Lang, *Heaven A History*. New Haven and London: Yale University Press., 1988.

McGeady, Sister Mary Rose. *"Am I Going to Heaven?"* United States of America: Covenant House, 1994.

Morse, Joseph Laffan, Sc.B., LL.B., LL.D. (Ed.) *The Universal Standard Encyclopedia* (Vol. 25). New York: Standard Reference Works Publishing Company, Inc., 1956.

Nageleisen, Rev. John A. *Charity for the Suffering Souls*. Rockford, Illinois: TAN Books and Publishers, Inc., 1982.

New American Bible, The, Catholic Bible Publishers, Wichita; Kansas. (1984-85 edition).

O'Sullivan, Fr. Paul, O.P. (E.D.M.) *How to Avoid Purgatory.* Rockford, Illinois: TAN Books and Publishers, Inc., 1992.

Panati, Charles. *Sacred Origins of Profound Things.* New York, New York: Penguin Books, USA., Inc., 1996.

Parente, Fr. Alessio, O.F.M. Cap. *The Holy Souls "Viva Padre Pio".* Barto, Pennsylvania: National Centre for Padre Pio, Inc., 1990.

Petrisko, Thomas W. *Call of the Ages.* Santa Barbara, California: Queenship Publishing Company, 1996.

Petrisko, Thomas W. *The Fatima Prophecies: At the Doorstep of the World.* McKees Rocks, Pennsylvania: St. Andrew's Productions, 1998.

Petrisko, Thomas W. *The Sorrow, The Sacrifice, and the Triumph: The Apparitions, Visions and Prophecies of Christina Gallagher.* New York: Simon & Schuster, Inc., 1995.

Polley, Jane (ed.) *Quest for the Past.* Pleasantville, N.Y.: Reader's Digest Association, Inc., 1984.

Ruffin, C. Bernard. *Padre Pio: The True Story.* Huntingdon, Indiana: Our Sunday Visitor, Inc., 1991.

Russell, Jeffrey Burton. *A History of Heaven.* Princeton, New Jersey: Princeton University Press, 1997.

Schmoger, Very Rev. Carl E., C.SS.R. *The Life of Anne Catherine Emmerich - Volume 1-2.* Rockford, Illinois: TAN Books and Publishers, Inc., 1976.

Schmoger, Very Rev. Carl E., C.SS.R. (ed.) *The Life of Jesus Christ and*

Biblical Revelations - Vols. 1-4 (From the Visions of the Venerable Anne Catherine Emmerich as Recorded by the Journals of Clemens Brentano) Rockford, Illinois: TAN Books and Publishers, Inc., 1979.

Schouppe, Fr. F.X., S.J. *Purgatory*. Rockford, Illinois: TAN Books and Publishers, Inc., 1986.

Suarez, Federico. *The Afterlife Death, Judgement, Heaven and Hell*. Manila, Phillippines: Sinag-tala Publishers, Inc., 1986 (English translation).

----. *The Catechism of the Council of Trent*. Rockford, Illinois: TAN Books and Publishers, Inc., 1982,

----. *The Spiritual Doctrine of Saint Catherine of Genoa*. Rockford, Illinois: TAN Books and Publishers, Inc., 1989.

Thurston, Herbert J., S.J. and Donald Attwater (eds.) *Butler's Lives of the Saints - Volume IV*. Allen, Texas: Christian Classics, 1996.

Turner, Alice K. *The History of Hell*. San Diego, California: Harcourt Brace & Company, 1993.

von Cochem, Fr. Martin, O.S.FC. *The Four Last Things - Death Judgment Hell Heaven*. Rockford, Illinois: TAN Books and Publishers, Inc., 1987.

Wales, Sean, C.SS.R. *The Last Things*. Liguori, Missouri: Publications, 1993.

Williams, Fr. Thomas David. *A Textual Concordance of the Holy Scriptures*. Rockford, Illinois: TAN Books and Publishers, Inc.

Copyright © 2001 St. Andrew's Productions. All World Rights Reserved

THE THIRD SECRET OF FATIMA VISION

Special Edition Prints Available!

Prayer Card	$ 1.00	*Includes Shipping*
8 x 10" Print Only	$ 5.00	+ $2.00 S/H
8 x 10" Gold Frame	$26.00	+ $6.00 S/H
12 x 16" Print Only	$ 8.00	+ $4.00 S/H
12 x 16" Gold Frame	$50.00	+ $10.00 S/H

20 x 24" Gicleé Gold Framed Print on 100% cotton paper,
$200 + Call for Shipping/Insurance

TO ORDER CALL: 1-412-787-9735
PLEASE CALL FOR QUANTITY PURCHASES

Help Spread the '*Queen of Peace*' Newspaper!

1 copy - $3.00	**TO ORDER CALL - 412-787-9791**
25 copies - $20.00	
50 copies - $36.00	Order the *Queen of Peace* Newspapers in Quantity and Save!
100 copies - $60.00	*Prices Include Shipping and Handling*
Over 100 copies - Call	★ *Newspaper Special* ★
★*Complete Set - $12.00*★	*Order the Complete Set for Only $12*

Secret of Fatima Edition

This 2001 edition takes a closer look at the Secret of Fatima, and in particular, the 'Third Secret' which was revealed by the Church on June 26, 2000. Included is the commentary written by Cardinal Ratzinger, which accompanied the secret's release.

Afterlife Edition

This edition examines the actual places of Heaven, Hell and Purgatory through the eyes of the Saints, Mystics,Visionaries, and Blessed Mother herself. Will you be ready come judgment day?

Illumination Edition

This edition focuses on a coming'day of enlightenment' in which every person on earth will see their souls in the same light that God sees them. Commonly referred to as the 'Warning' or 'Mini-Judgment', many saints and visionaries, particularly the Blessed Mother have spoken about this great event, now said to be imminent.

Eternal Father Edition

This edition makes visible the love and tenderness of God the Father and introduces a special consecration to Him. Many of His messages for the world today tell of the great love He has for all of His 'Prodigal Children.'

Holy Spirit Edition

This edition reveals how the Holy Spirit continues to work through time and history, raising up great saints in the Church. Emphasized in the hidden, yet important role of St. Joseph.

Eucharistic Edition

This edition contains evidence for the Real Presence of Christ in the Eucharist. Many miracles and messages are recorded to reaffirm this truth.

Special Edition III

This edition focuses on the great prophecies the Blessed Mother has given to the world since her apparitions in 1917 at Fatima. Prophetic events related to the 'Triumph of Her Immaculate Heart' are addressed in detail.

Special Edition II

This edition examines the apparitions of the Blessed Mother at Fatima and in relation to today's apparitions occurring worldwide.

Special Edition I

The first in a trilogy of the apparitions and messages of the Blessed Mother, this edition tells why Mary has come to earth and is appearing to all parts of the world today.

Best Sellers by Dr. Thomas W. Petrisko!

Inside Heaven and Hell

What History, Theology and Mystics Tell Us About the Afterlife
Take a spiritual journey with the saints, mystics, visionaries, and the Blessed Mother – inside Heaven and Hell! Discover what really happens at your judgment. With profound new insight into what awaits each one of us, this book is a ***must read for all those who are serious about earning their 'salvation.'*** **$ 14.95**

The Miracle of the Illumination of All Consciences

Known as the 'Warning' or 'Mini-Judgment' a coming "day of enlightenment" has been foretold. It is purported to be a day in which God will supernaturally illuminate the conscience of every man, woman, and child on earth. Each person, then, would momentarily see the state of their soul through God's eyes and realize the truth of His existence. **$12.95**

The Fatima Prophecies

At the Doorstep of the World
This powerhouse book tells of the many contemporary prophecies and apparitions and how they point to the fulfillment of Fatima's two remaining prophecies, the 'annihilation of nations' and 'era of peace'. Is the world about to enter the era of peace or will there be a terrible chastisement? Contains over 60 pictures. **$14.95**

Fatima's Third Secret Explained

Officially made public to the world on June 26, 2000, the controversial *Third Secret* of Fatima is not easily understood. This work seeks to explain the *Third Secret* in the context of the entire message of Fatima and decipher what it might mean for the world today. Included is the invaluable commentary written by Cardinal Ratzinger which accompanied the secrets release. The book also contains a photocopy of the original *Third Secret* text written in Sr. Lucia's own handwriting. **$14.99**

Toll-Free (888) 654-6279 or (412) 787-9735 www.SaintAndrew.com

St. Andrew's Productions Order Form

Order Toll-Free! 1-888-654-6279 or 1-412-787-9735
Visa, MasterCard Accepted!

_____ Call of the Ages (Petrisko)	$12.95
_____ Catholic Answers for Catholic Parents	$ 8.95
_____ Catholic Parents Internet Guide	$ 3.00
_____ Face of the Father, The (Petrisko)	$ 9.95
_____ False Prophets of Today (Petrisko)	$ 7.95
_____ Fatima Prophecies, The (Petrisko)	$14.95
_____ Fatima's Third Secret Explained (Petrisko)	$14.99
_____ Finding Our Father (Centilli)	$ 4.95
_____ Glory to the Father (Petrisko)	$ 8.95
_____ God 2000 (Fr. Richard Foley, SJ)	$11.95
_____ Holy Spirit in the Writings of PJP II	$19.95
_____ In God's Hands (Petrisko)	$12.95
_____ Inside Heaven and Hell (Petrisko)	$14.95
_____ Inside Purgatory (Petrisko)	$10.95
_____ Kingdom of Our Father, The (Petrisko)	$16.95
_____ Last Crusade, The (Petrisko)	$ 9.95
_____ Mary in the Church Today (McCarthy)	$14.95
_____ Miracle of the Illumination, The	$12.95
_____ Prophecy of Daniel, The (Petrisko)	$ 7.95
_____ Prodigal Children, The (Centilli)	$ 4.95
_____ Seeing with the Eyes of the Soul: Vol. 1	$ 3.00
_____ Seeing with the Eyes of the Soul: Vol. 2	$ 3.00
_____ Seeing with the Eyes of the Soul: Vol. 3	$ 3.00
_____ Seeing with the Eyes of the Soul: Vol. 4	$ 3.00
_____ Sorrow, Sacrifice and the Triumph	$13.00
_____ St. Joseph and the Triumph (Petrisko)	$10.95

Queen of Peace Newspapers
_____ *Afterlife Edition* (Heaven, Hell and Purgatory) **$3.00ea.**

Name:_____

Address:_____

City:_____St_____Zip_____

Phone:_____Fax_____

Visa/MasterCard_____

Total Enclosed:_____

PLEASE ADD SHIPPING/TAX
$0-24.99...$4.00, $25-49.99...$6.00, $50-99.99...$8.00, $100 + Add 8%
PA Residents Add 7% Tax
OR MAIL ORDER TO:
St. Andrew's Productions, 6111 Steubenville Pike, McKees Rocks, PA 15136
www.SaintAndrew.com

CPSIA information can be obtained
at www.ICGtesting.com
Printed in the USA
JSHW012355090920
7746JS00001B/70